Put Your Psychic Powers to Work:
A Practical Guide to Parapsychology

Put Your Psychic Powers

evelyn monahan

with

terry bakken

Nelson-Hall

to Work:

a practical guide
to parapsychology

Company, Chicago

Second Printing, 1974

ISBN 0-88229-132-7

Library of Congress Catalog Card No. 73-84208

Nelson-Hall Company, Publishers
325 Jackson Boulevard, Chicago, Illinois 60606

Manufactured in the United States of America.

To Betty C. Reaid,
who has been the greatest source
of inspiration and encouragement
to Evelyn Monahan.

To the four children of Terry Bakken—
Shari, Jim, Lori, and Karen—
who will grow up to inherit a world
made better through the science of parapsychology.

Contents

Foreword

The purpose of this book is to make available to its readers factual knowledge concerning parapsychology and psychic phenomena. In addition to simple facts, presented here are proven methods which an individual may use to develop his own psychic abilities—for these abilities are not the gifts of a chosen few, but belong to each of us, as an integral part of our own human nature.

In the course of teaching parapsychology at Georgia State University, and during the years of study prior to my teaching experience, I became very aware that the great majority of books dealing with parapsychology, E.S.P., and psychic phenomena related only the personal experiences of an individual and did nothing to actually teach a reader to get in touch with his own abilities. This is not such a book. The exercises included here have been researched and have proven extremely effective under actual learning conditions for more than two years. They are not magic formulas but techniques founded in science and educational psychology which will enable a person to expand his own potential.

If a reader is seeking absolute truths and guaranteed panaceas, this is not the book for him. Information is presented here with an attitude of respect for an individual's right to reach his own conclusions. It is my opinion that each individual has an obligation to acquaint himself with facts that will enable him to reach those conclusions, based upon knowledge, not emotion. It is not my purpose to convince, but to stimulate intellectual curiosity and to provide the methods for developing individual abilities. It is through this intellectual curiosity that human potential can be recognized and expanded.

So let us embark upon this journey together, for as a very wise man said centuries ago, "The beginning of wisdom is wonder!"

Put Your Psychic Powers to Work:
A Practical Guide to Parapsychology

1 Clairvoyance and Psychometry

Clairvoyance has fascinated mankind for centuries. The literal definition of clairvoyance is clear-seeing or clear-sight. The term clairvoyance encompasses not only future but also past events and those that occur at the same moment and time but at a different location.

In order to fully evaluate clairvoyance as a potential ability inherent in man it is necessary to look at past teachings about the subject and at scientific investigations still being carried on in the field. The ancients were aware that a select few had the ability to look into the future. Yoga has taught for centuries that man can set aside his conscious mind and put himself in tune with the so-called universal unconscious or cosmic mind. Yoga also postulated the existence of the Akashic records, which were considered to be a universal ether that held the recorded happenings of an entire world cycle—not just the past but also present and future. Yogis teach that an advanced clairvoyant or others who possess occult powers of this kind can tune themselves in with the universal ether and "read" past, present, and future of an entire world cycle. They believe that the records terminate only with the ending of the particular world cycle to which they refer.

In Greek history much belief in the Oracle of Delphi was expressed. The Oracle, considered a high priestess, was consulted by many rulers in connection with personal events, wars, and strategies for battle. Hippocrates, the father of medicine, once wrote, "The affliction suffered by the body, the soul sees with shut eyes."

Today we are witnessing a new emphasis— new not only in time but also in that scientists are becoming interested in clairvoyance. The list of those who have investigated the subject is impressive and growing continuously. Dr. William McDougall, who taught at Harvard and Oxford, was responsible for bringing Dr. J. B. Rhine and his wife Dr. Louisa Rhine to Duke University in the 1920s to study and experiment with paranormal happenings. Books and magazines today report the work of Russian scientists related to clairvoyance and other areas of parapsychology. The Czechoslovakian journal *Periscope*, 1966, states that the Czech military in 1925 issued to its army a handbook, *Clairvoyance, Hypnotism, and Magnetism,* by Karl Hejbalik.

Usually it is easy to accept the possibility of somehow looking ahead in time to predict a future event. It is often somewhat more difficult to accept that one who has developed his inherent clairvoyant abilities can also reach into the past, perhaps into an event long forgotten, and give specific information about a specific event in a person's life. The idea that the past is a dead issue is challenged as someone sensitive to the past reaches back even into the early years of childhood and describes in detail the person's home at the time of the event, colors in the home, medical history, and conversations that may have occurred 20, 30, or more years ago.

That this sort of description has in fact happened and is continuing to happen confronts man's conception of time itself. Einstein has said that time is relative. Time zones divide the world, and United States residents each year through the institution of daylight saving time, intervene and order events by changing time itself for a particular duration. If time is indeed relative and merely a matter of a man-made intervention to record events in their order of occurrence, it is not difficult to accept that the mind is capable of transcending time itself.

To consider clairvoyance in general, the reader must acquaint himself with the idea that the universe is filled with objects and happenings that vibrate at different frequencies. Microwave ovens, which cook food in a matter of seconds by means of sound vibrations, are a concrete example of the existence of vibrations. The human brain itself operates and emits electrical magnetic impulses—impulses that are released into the surrounding atmosphere and held captive by the material objects they contact. The student is here reminded that every object, no matter how solid it may appear to the observer, is in essence composed of millions of atoms, electrons, neutrons, and neutrinos. Unoccupied space exists in even the most apparently solid object.

Clairvoyance thus seems to be more intimately tied with physics and electrical engineering than with psychology. To discover the natural laws responsible for the operations of phenomena now considered extrasensory we must look to these sciences as well as to the nature of the human mind. In attempting to explain clairvoyant ability we may compare the brain, emitting electrical magnetic impulses, to a radio. That is, one might tune in to various frequencies much as one turns a radio dial to select a specific station. The law of conservation of energy states that energy can be neither created nor destroyed, but merely changes from one form to another. If this law is accepted as fact, it again becomes easier to conceive of the mind's ability to tune itself through various techniques and to tap energies released into our atmosphere even centuries ago.

That a furnace in operation emits heat is easily determined by opening the furnace door.

When the furnace is down, heat remains in the room, even though its initiating cause is no longer present. So we see once again that effects released into our surrounding atmosphere linger and can be perceived even when the initiating cause is no longer present.

One of the easiest methods of triggering clairvoyance in any individual is the technique of psychometry. Psychometry, sometimes known as object reading, is based on the idea that over long periods of time, even centuries, vibrations are absorbed and held by material objects. Bear in mind that an object will contain not only the vibrations of its owner but also the vibrations of those people who are significant in the owner's life. It is possible with psychometry, as with ordinary clairvoyance, to travel backward into a person's childhood to deal with the present life period or to travel forward into the person's future.

That the vibrations of significant others in the owner's life are also found on an object is sometimes puzzling to one who ventures for the first time into this field. One must consider here the possibility that in any meaningful relationship there is an exchange of vibrational energy. One becomes in part identified with the significant person. To some extent one's own essence in the vibrational field becomes colored by a meaningful exchange with another person.

Psychometry, however, not only is possible with objects of possession but also can be induced by the use of a person's full name and through such personal contact as hand holding. In each case it can be said that the person is presented with the loose end of the string that guides him into the past, present, and future. Occult teachers speak of the Aka thread, which can be visualized through the analogy of a spider that weaves a web as it moves from object to object. These threads are thought to be lines of communication, much like an index file in a library, which can direct a person to the information he seeks.

Several important facts must be kept in mind in regard to psychometry as a means of tapping clairvoyant ability. First, and most important, is the length of time the object has been associated with its owner and whether the owner has been the sole possessor of the object. Complications can arise if the object has belonged to several different people, any of whom is not well known to the present owner. A person who uses the object as a point of contact might very well pick up extremely accurate and specific events recorded on the object —say, a wristwatch or a ring—through the vibrations of the previous owner. If the present wearer of the jewelry is not well acquainted with details in the previous owner's life, accurate and specific information may be passed over as incorrect; so it is best to choose an object that has been associated only with the person for whom a clairvoyant demonstration is being attempted.

Second, a person who uses clairvoyant ability

with or without the aid of an object is confronted with the problems of interpretation. Impressions come in many different ways. One person may see pictures; another may see symbols; others may hear voices; others report knowledge through feelings. Any combination of these various forms of receiving impressions can be expected. Often the information is received so quickly that while the sensitive is relating one incident in a person's life, another impression has already completely formed in the mind's eye.

The process is further complicated in that close emotional relationships are difficult to distinguish from actual blood ties. Then add that strong desires are often indistinguishable from a feat accomplished, and it becomes easier to see that proficient interpretation itself takes time and practice.

Psychometry is particularly advantageous in attempting a clairvoyance demonstration with a particular person in a crowded room. Remember that every person in the room is giving off vibrational energy; so the use of an object that belongs to the involved person acts as a focusing device, making it easier to ignore crosscurrents of vibrations from everyone else in the room.

If psychometry is to be done through the use of a name rather than an object, the complete name should be used—for example, John Joseph Smith, Jr. A married woman should include her maiden name—for example, Mary Anne Kelly Jones. Confusion can result when a junior or senior designation is not included in the name given to the person who is attempting the demonstration. Such omission results usually in specific information being picked up on both father and son. Keep in mind that the closer the emotional tie or the more significant the other, the stronger will be the significant other's vibrational effect in the subject's own energy field.

Photographs also afford a means of inducing clairvoyance through psychometry. It is interesting to note here that many primitive tribes would not permit photographs to be taken in the belief that the camera captured part of the individual's soul. When dealing with photographs it is not necessary that the sensitive see the picture. The picture may be handed to him face down and merely held between both hands in order to receive information. Keep in mind that information will be picked up on every person present in the photograph, on the significant people in their lives, and often on the person who took the picture. Actual description of the photograph's content is also possible in these cases.

Many times the subject cannot directly relate to information given, and he must ask people closely associated with him to aid in possible verification. In all cases, specific information and verification of facts is of utmost importance. To deal in generalities is to demonstrate nothing in the field of clairvoyant investigation. Whenever possible, demonstrations should be recorded on tape and/or written for a later verification. In no instance should facts be twisted or otherwise turned back in order to fit a situation or event in the subject's life.

No profession today can claim absolute perfection, and it is not possible in the area of clairvoyance. The person who performs a clairvoyant demonstration would do well to remember and remind those present during the demonstration that when dealing in such a specific manner with clairvoyant events in a person's life the odds are not 1 in 10, 1 in 100, or even 1 in 1,000. When dealing in specifics—for example, "Your left lower leg was broken at the age of seven years in a fall down the front steps of your aunt's home"—the odds are one in infinity.

The clairvoyant should instruct all subjects and observers present to make no remarks either in word or through body language—for example, facial gestures, looks of surprise—until the clairvoyant has completely finished with the information he intends to convey for verification. The clairvoyant should not look at the subject as he relates the clairvoyant impressions received. The less the subject and observers say before the demonstration, the better. Be on your guard against any supposed clairvoyant who plies you with questions and watches your every move for any sign of reaction during the demonstration. In the interest of scientific investigation every precaution must be taken to ensure that information received and labeled as clairvoyant knowledge could not have been conveyed by any ordinarily accepted means of communication.

It is quite difficult to demonstrate past-time clairvoyance with a subject the demonstrator has known well for an extended period of time. The clairvoyant then must endeavor to pick up on a time period and give minute details in order to dispel any doubt about possible discussion of these events prior to the demonstration. It is always much easier to demonstrate clairvoyance with someone who is not known at all or whose past life is not known.

When dealing with future time, clairvoyance, or precognition, this lack of knowledge about past events is not so important. In all precognitive demonstrations the time period should be pinpointed as closely as possible and the event described specifically and not in generalities. For verification of future-time clairvoyance the subject might be requested to advise the clairvoyant when the predicted time period has passed whether the event actually did occur. The clairvoyant, too, should retain a record of the events predicted, including the time in which they were to occur. Then the clairvoyant can check with the subject in order to maintain a more accurate record of hits and misses.

Clairvoyance Exercises

CLAIRVOYANCE USING ESP CARDS

The ESP deck (available from the Foundation for Research into the Nature of Man, Durham, N.C.) consists of 25 cards with 5 symbols: circle, plus (+) sign, star, 3 wavy lines, square. Each symbol appears on five cards in the deck.

Down-through Method

In this exercise the cards are shuffled and cut three times with a metal edge. The deck then is placed aside, and on a sheet of paper, prepared in advance, the subject notes with numbers from 1 to 25, the order in which he feels the symbols are arranged in the deck. For accuracy at least four runs should be completed. Statistically one may expect to have five hits by chance. The amount of deviation from five will be a measure of the amount of clairvoyant ability being evidenced. After four runs have been completed the subject should add the number of hits in each run. Chance expectations of hits for the 4 runs is 20; so approximately 28 hits would be quite in excess of the 20-to-1 odds. If the subject has scored 32 or more hits in the 4 runs he has attained chance occurrence odds of 250 to 1.

For his convenience the subject should divide a page into columns. The left-hand column is headed *Call*; the right-hand column is headed *Card*. The subject notes his impressions of the symbols in the deck, 1 through 25, in the Call column. Then he goes through the deck one card at a time, noting the symbols in their actual order of appearance, 1 through 25, in the Card column. This method allows for speedy verification. (Pre-printed forms may be obtained from the Foundation for Research into the Nature of Man, Durham, N.C.)

Basic Technique

The subject shuffles the deck, which then should be cut three times with a metal edge. The subject uses the prepared sheet as mentioned above. After the deck has been shuffled and set aside, the subject removes the top card from the deck and places it to the side of the stack without looking at its face. The subject then attempts to identify the symbol on the card and records it on his performance sheet in the Call column. The second card should be taken from the deck in the same manner but not placed on top of the preceding card until the subject has attempted his identification and reported his impression on his performance sheet. This method is used until the subject has gone through all 25 cards and recorded his impressions. After the second impression has been recorded, the second card may be placed on top of the first card drawn so that the subject amasses a second stack of cards. After all impressions have been recorded, the subject turns over the new stack of cards and records the actual appearance of the symbols in the Card column. Since the deck has been turned over, the cards will appear face up in their order of appearance 1 through 25. When four runs have been completed the odds given above also will apply here.

General ESP

This experiment involves two or more people. The deck is shuffled and cut as before. One person handles the deck while the other or others record his impressions. Since this technique can involve both clairvoyance and telepathy, the person designated to handle the deck is called the sender.

The sender takes one card at a time from the deck and holds it so that only he can physically see the symbol on the card. The sender holds a mental image of this symbol in his mind for 10 seconds. The subject records his impressions; then the sender picks up the next card from the deck and follows the same procedure as with the first card drawn. To indicate the progression to the subject the sender simply says, "number two," before he begins to hold his mental impression for 10 seconds. The second card drawn is then placed face down on top of the preceding card. The third card is drawn and its number (three) announced, and the visual image of the symbol is again held for 10 seconds. The third card is then placed face down on the two preceding cards. This procedure continues until the sender has announced number 25 and the subject has recorded his impression. Then the sender turns over the newly formed stack and states aloud the actual appearance of the symbols—for example, number one, square; number two, circle—while the subject records this order in his Card column. Again after four runs the number of hits in each run is added and performance gauged according to the statistical information given above.

In the first two exercises clairvoyance alone is being tested, since no one has seen the actual order of the symbols in the deck. In the third exercise telepathy or clairvoyance may be responsible for hits above chance, since the sender is holding a mental image of the symbol as it appears on the card.

Techniques to Facilitate Clairvoyance and Telepathy with ESP Cards

1. Breath technique is extremely important. Subjects should inhale a deep breath, extending the diaphragm, and visualize the breath's traveling to the area of the pineal gland (on the forehead

between and just above the eyebrows.) This breath technique should be repeated three times before a subject attempts to record any impressions.

2. Some subjects may find it helpful to close their eyes and visualize a projection screen. Then the symbol would appear on the screen.

3. It can be beneficial to gaze at the deck and, in the first exercise, to mentally extend one's sight to actually pass through the cards and see or feel the images on their faces. In the first exercise the sight is extended one card at a time, after the impression of the previous card has been recorded. The same technique may be used in the second exercise, but here it is necessary to extend the sight through only one card at a time.

In the third exercise both sender and subject perform the preliminary breathing exercises. The sender takes an additional deep breath each time he draws a card from the deck and holds its mental image in his mind. The subject then may be aided by visualizing the image of the symbol as actually falling into his head. A helpful technique in distinguishing among the five symbols is the use of extended sensory perception to be aware of the feeling each symbol imparts. Squares tend to feel heavy; circles tend to feel light; stars tend to feel sharp or pointed; wavy lines convey the feeling of movement; plus signs convey a combination of sharpness with empty space. With practice the subject will become aware of how each symbol mentally feels to him; then his number of hits above chance will increase greatly. Extended sensory perception is the key here as in all clairvoyant, telepathic, and psychometric techniques.

ESP WITH REGULAR PLAYING CARDS

From a regular deck of playing cards the four aces are removed and placed side by side across the top of the table. The subject shuffles the remaining 48 cards and then cuts the deck 3 times with a metal edge. Then he selects the top card and places it to one side of the deck, face down. Using the techniques of extended sensory perception he attempts to place this card by suit on the proper ace; for example, if his impression is that the card is a diamond he places the card face down under the ace of diamonds, forming a column as he adds cards. This procedure is continued, a card at a time, until the subject has matched all 48 cards with their respective aces. Two complete trials or runs through the deck are necessary to attain statistical significance. When the subject has completed the run by placing the 48 cards in columns, he then turns the cards over, a column at a time; for example, all cards under the ace of diamonds column are turned over and hits recorded as the number of diamonds actually placed in the column. Each column is recorded in the same way.

When the numbers of hits in 2 runs have been recorded they are added together and evaluated according to the following statistics for 2 runs: chance score for 2 runs is 96 cards with 24 hits; 32 hits will yield odds of 20 to 1. Hits of 35 and above yield the odds of 100 to 1 of their occurrence by chance alone.

Techniques to Aid the Subject

The preliminary breathing techniques noted in the previous exercises also apply here. Through extended sensory perception the subject can learn to be aware of the distinct differences in the four suits. Red has a light, warm feeling. Black has a heavy, slightly depressing feeling; diamonds and spades have a sharp feeling when touched through extended sensory perception. To distinguish between a diamond and a spade one must be aware of the feeling of lightness or heaviness associated with the feeling of sharpness. Hearts and clubs have a rounded or smooth feeling. Again the subject must consider the lightness or heaviness associated with the extended feeling of roundness or smoothness. With practice the subject will find that he can become quite proficient at distinguishing a suit of cards face down.

PSYCHOMETRIC CLAIRVOYANCE
(Clairvoyance stimulated through psychometry while holding an object)

1. Hold the object between the hands. A watch or a ring is often the best object for use in

psychometric demonstrations because its association with the subject usually has been of long duration and daily contact. Take three deep breaths, extending the diaphragm with each and visualizing the breath concentrated in the pineal gland area (between and just above the eyebrows). Remember to relax the stomach muscles after each breath.

2. Do not look at the subject or get any feedback until the demonstration is completely finished.

3. Speak your impressions without censorship. (Someone should already have been designated to record your spoken impressions in writing; then you can verify them at the conclusion of the demonstration.) It is extremely important that your first impressions, no matter how silly they may seem to you, be spoken without the intervention of logical reasoning. When logical reasoning enters, the state of altered consciousness associated with clairvoyance leaves. The first impressions you receive may deal with various senses and may present themselves to you in various ways.

When the free flow of impressions stops, it is time to mentally extend your senses for specific information. For example, if a description of the person's home has not come during the free flow period of impressions, mentally ask yourself to be aware of this person's home. Extend your sense of sight to be aware of architecture, furniture arrangement, color, pictures on the walls, and any unusual object in the room. Speak these impressions as quickly as they come to you. If the person seems to have a purple sofa with orange polka dots and yellow stripes, say it. Do not let yourself reason that no one in his right mind would own such a sofa. You may be surprised at how many seemingly ridiculous impressions are validated on completion of the demonstration.

4. Next extend other senses to receive specific information about other questions. The senses of hearing, taste, smell, and touch may be extended exactly as was the sense of sight. For example, if you want to know what the subject's favorite food is you should mentally ask yourself the question, extending your sense of smell and taste to obtain the desired information. You may experience a very salty or a very sweet or sour taste in your mouth. You may also find that associated with the salty taste in your mouth is the feeling of something brittle on your tongue. The impression formed from these sensations may be that the subject delights in potato chips. If you find it difficult to imagine anyone's delight in potato chips you again should not allow logical reasoning or personal preference to enter the situation.

5. You may want information about a specific period in the subject's life. For example, although you are an adult you may want information specific to the subject during his eighth year of life. In this situation extend your senses through time, remembering that whatever has been is never

completely lost. Ask yourself mentally what specific events had particular impact for the subject at age eight. A free flow period of impressions may follow this mental question. Relate this information as it occurs. Now ask yourself mentally to be aware of the subject's home during his eight years. Extend all the senses as above. This technique of mental questioning for specific information can be carried on indefinitely.

6. Past medical history often is a valuable area in which to demonstrate the specificity of this technique. Mentally ask yourself for information about the subject's physical, emotional, and mental state as it was in the past and as it exists now. Free flow information will follow. Then you may want to ask the mental question: "Does this person have any scars or identifiable marks that are covered by garments?" If you want medical information from a particular period of life you need only ask the mental question: "What was this person's physical, emotional, and mental state during his 21st year."

7. As should be evident by now, information may be as detailed and specific as you desire simply by asking delineated mental questions of yourself and extending your senses in order to be aware of the answers.

2 Telepathy

Almost every human being at some time has experienced spontaneous telepathy. The incident may have involved two people who spoke identical words at the same moment. Or a person may have thought about someone, received a telephone call, and found that the caller was the very party being thought about.

The idea that one mind can communicate with another mind or, indeed, with many minds simultaneously has enchanted and mystified man since the beginning of reported history. Creative writers, writers of science fiction, and poets often have used as a theme the ideal form of communication, mind-to-mind contact, without a word spoken.

Science has explored the idea of telepathy with the aid of modern scientific instruments such as the electroencephalograph. The Russians have succeeded in demonstrating telepathy between two people, one in Moscow and the other in Leningrad. Scientists in Russia also have been able to show by means of the electroencephalograph the exact moment a telepathic communication leaves the sender and the exact moment it enters the mind of the receiver.

What telepathy has to offer mankind is the possibility that one day the deaf and the mute may be able to communicate telepathically. For those who are able to speak their thoughts and hear spoken communications telepathy offers the possibility of an open line of communication in times of emergency as well as in everyday life.

The effectiveness of involving the senses in telepathic communication has been proven over a two-year period in classes and experimentation conducted at Georgia State University in Atlanta, Georgia. Various techniques were used to evaluate learning conditions conducive to both sending and receiving telepathic communication. These techniques began with the sender's merely sending a word, a book title, or a playing card from an ordinary deck of 52 cards, and gradually involved the senses in sequential order.

For example, beginning experiments merely required that the sender concentrate on the word *flower*. Then the sender not only attempted to communicate the word *flower*, but also to include a specific image of a red rose. The addition of the red rose image to the thought of the word *flower* was found to be more readily received.

As each new sense was involved in the message to be communicated, accuracy of reception increased phenomenally. The end product, a message sent telepathically, using each of the ordinarily accepted senses, might be as follows. The sender, wanting to convey the mental image of a flower to one or more subjects, would envision a red rose so that it could be clearly seen in the mind's eye. He would add to this the fragrance associated with roses in full bloom, then would mentally run his hand very lightly over the blossom so as to include in his mental image the softness and the thorns associated with roses. In order to involve the senses of hearing and taste the sender would mentally recall the sound of bees hovering above a garden of roses and would mentally touch a rose petal to his tongue.

Full use of all the senses energizes a telepathic message, and it finds its way to the receiver telepathically through five doors simultaneously. The greater the bombardment and involvement of the senses with which the receiver is well acquainted, the greater is the accuracy of the receiver in telepathic reception.

Telepathic experiments have not been confined to human subjects. Dr. Karlis Osis worked extensively with telepathy in cats, and one of Dr. J. B. Rhine's first research endeavors in parapsychology involved a horse who was alleged to have telepathic ability. Interestingly, Dr. Rhine and his associates could find no logical explanation for the way the animal followed mental commands, and they were left with telepathy as the sole means of interpreting the animal's behavior.

Since the reader has already learned that the brain works on electrical impulses, the idea that thought is actually patterned energy should not be too difficult to accept. The human mind seems capable of sending thought over a great distance or to someone in the same room. Here it must be kept in mind that to validate telepathic communication one must be able to rule out the possibility of any ordinary sensory cues. Insistence on a strict scientific framework cannot be overemphasized. All telepathic experiments must be prefaced with practical means of excluding any possibility of communication other than that of mind to mind.

In telepathy as in clairvoyance and psychometry it is important that the reader realize he is doing no more than extending his normally accepted senses. In fact, when sending a telepathic message the more the sender is able to involve his senses in the thought he wants to communicate, the easier it will be for the receiver to pick up and interpret the message.

Telepathy Exercises

1. This exercise can involve two or any number of people. The person selected as sender takes the receivers on an imaginary trip. He states aloud, "I am going to take you on a shopping trip," or "I'm going to take you to a place that means a great deal to me."

The sender then speaks a line, leaving a blank statement for the receivers to fill in on receipt of a telepathic message. For example, "I am going into a certain type store. As I enter the store I am particularly aware of the fragrance that seems to permeate the surroundings. I am going to experience this fragrance and communicate it to you. Extend your senses with me and write down with no communication among you the fragrance you feel I am attempting to convey to you." "I am now walking through the store. My eye is caught by a particular article; the color impresses me and I touch the article. I will now communicate to you through thought the color and texture I am experiencing." "Extend your sight and sense of touch and share in my experience. As before, with no communication among yourselves, write down your impressions."

This exercise may be continued to include 10 separate experiences in the imaginary journey. In each experience the reader should attempt to involve as many of the senses as possible.

2. This exercise also can involve two or any number of persons. They can be in the same room or can be physically removed from the sender by any distance. The exercise involves telepathic communication of a drawing or sketch, which the receiver is to duplicate.

Simple geometric figures may be used at first. Easy items, such as a cup and saucer or a house, also may be used. The idea here is for the receiver to duplicate as closely as possible the sketch that the sender is drawing and communicating. As greater proficiency is developed more detailed drawings may be used. For example, instead of using a simplified picture of a house the sender may put in a certain number of windows, trees surrounding the house, or a specific kind of door on the house. The experiment's success again will be determined by how closely the receiver's sketch resembles the sender's original sketch.

3. This exercise involves the use of a deck of ordinary playing cards. Once the deck has been shuffled and cut the sender takes the top card and attempts to convey to his receiver or receivers the number and suit of the selected card. Again the senses must be brought into play.

Through experimentation it has been found

that people perceive the color red as weighing less than black. Thus the receiver could distinguish between the two colors by allowing himself to be aware of lightness or heaviness.

In determining the suit of the card it has been shown that hearts and clubs are experienced as rounded objects. A heart may be distinguished from a club by the degree of heaviness involved with the round shape. Diamonds and spades are experienced as pointed objects, a feeling of sharpness. Here again the degree of heaviness involved allows the receiver to distinguish the suit. Face cards are experienced as crowded patterns, a feeling of fullness.

Once the receiver has determined that a face card is involved he need only return to the before-mentioned exercise for distinguishing the suit. It is suggested that this exercise be done with all 52 cards. If the participants do not have time to run through the entire deck, the deck should be placed aside in two stacks—one stack for the cards already sent and placed in the order of their appearance, the other stack for unsent cards, which is placed aside without disturbing the order of the cards or looking at the cards to ascertain their order in the deck. Verification of the telepathic communication can not take place until the entire deck of 52 cards has been sent. Completion allows the statistics for any exact hit (king of hearts) to remain 1 in 52 and for 2 or more hits to be calculated easily from this base of chance expectation.

3 Human Aura

The human aura is a highly charged magnetic field that surrounds and permeates the human body. Although one can learn to see the aura within 5 or 10 minutes, most people are unaware of its existence, possibly because of functional blindness. People often see selectively in looking at an object; so they may be unaware of much of the detail in the object because they have attended only to certain features.

Much research related to the human aura has been done. Dr. Walter J. Kilner, physician at St. Thomas Hospital in London, did the first known scientific experiments in determining by laboratory means the nature of the aura. These experiments were begun in 1908, when Dr. Kilner first noticed a haze around the human body. He became interested in exploring the possibility that this haze or aura might reflect a person's physiological state, and he did, in fact, find that particular colors and patterns in the aura accompanied certain diseases in the body. In 1920 Dr. Kilner published his book, *Human Atmosphere*, which was followed by *Human Aura*. It was Dr. Kilner's opinion that 95 out of 100 people with unaided vision could be trained to see and interpret the aura.

In Russia a form of photography, the Kirlian method, has made it possible for scientists to photograph and evaluate the magnetic field that surrounds all living human beings. Recently at Stanford University American scientists have duplicated the Russian feat by photographing the human aura in color. Another researcher at Cornell, Dr. Otto Rahn, discovered after extensive research that the strongest human radiations emanate from the fingertips of the right hand. This finding has long been known to persons involved in psychic healing.

Evidence that the aura has been seen for centuries, although its exact nature was not known, can be found in religious paintings that depict halos around the bodies of saints and prophets. Thanks to the efforts of many researchers we are now able to make specific, verifiable statements about the human aura. The magnetic field that immediately surrounds the body and extends about one-eighth inch around all portions of the body, including the hair, usually is referred to as the etheric or bioplasmic body. This narrow band is sensitive to touch, and one can learn with little difficulty to be aware of its existence. Several researchers have found that this inner aura will respond to a magnet; it can be attracted to a magnet, but is not itself a magnet. So the aura does have mass, probably because of the presence of iron particles.

The aura extends farther around such projections as the nipples and the fingers than it does from flatter surfaces. It is interesting to note here that this state is also true of an electrically charged conductor.

Scientists in Russia, the United States, and England have found that it is possible to impart a beneficial thought, perhaps a slight charge of electrical energy, by means of the aura. The brighter a person's aura, the stronger the electrical charge he is able to convey to another. Using breath techniques an individual may learn to increase the energy in the aura and to direct it at will through and to a given point.

When one first becomes aware of the aura one possibly may not at the same time become aware of its various colors and patterns. The ability to see colors and patterns in the aura seems with many people to be a function of time and practice; others see color immediately; still others report awareness of the rainbow of light since childhood. Although the field of color interpretation related to the aura still needs much investigation and refinement, several statements can be made in regard to the relationship between the presence of certain colors and a person's physiological, emotional, and mental state. Most of the evidence gathered to date has been empirical; the area itself is open to much deeper investigation in the interpretation of particular shades and hues.

Some general interpretations for particular colors in the aura are the following. Red usually represents vitality and energy. It has been found experimentally that when a person becomes angry, red dominates the auric field. Blue correlates most often with philosophic pursuits. Much study still remains to be done in regard to specific shades of blue. Yellow correlates with such mental activity as logical reasoning and critical analysis. Black has been found to correlate with moods of malice, hatred, and severe depression. The color white requires considerably more investigation. Yogis and other occultists consider it to be indicative of a highly evolved being, such as a master or guru. Splotches of brown have been found around and near diseased organs, and gray seems to correlate with negative emotions such as fear, mild depression, and a generally negative attitude. Limey yellowish-green has been found to correlate with deceit. A restful, deep green often is seen around people who have a great love for the out-of-doors. The student must remember that much remains to be discovered about color and pattern in the human aura and how it relates to the human being in everyday life.

Human Aura Exercises

VIEWING THE AURA OF OTHERS

1. Select a room with an unpatterned wall.

2. Lighting should be enough to allow the people present in the room to distinguish the features of the person whose aura is to be viewed.

3. The viewers should look at the subject's forehead (subject positioned in front of a neutral wall). The viewers should allow their gazes to wander around the head and the rest of the body.

4. To enhance the energy in the aura the subject should be instructed to take a deep breath, being sure to extend the diaphragm as the breath is taken. The subject then should imagine and will the inhaled breath to the very top of the head. During this process the subject should relax the stomach muscles.

5. When the subject has taken the breath and willed it to the top of his head, viewers should concentrate their sight on the area of the head and particularly the crown of the head. The aura usually is seen as a fluctuating light mist or haze

(i.e., many people describe the aura's appearance as similar to heat waves that rise from the ground on a very hot day).

6. To further confirm that the energy pull in the aura can be controlled, while the viewers are concentrating on the crown of the head the subject should take another deep breath and again direct this breath to the scalp area. The viewers then should be able to see the increase in the brightness of the aura and to be aware of its fluctuation under the control of the will.

7. The subject should now extend his hand, palm facing the viewers, fingers pointed toward the ceiling. A deep breath should be taken as before, but this time the subject should imagine the breath concentrated in the hand. Viewers are instructed to be aware of the aura and its fluctuation, particularly at the fingertips.

8. Staring is not necessary and not encouraged. If a viewer has any doubt about what he is observing he should avert his eyes for a moment and then look again at the subject.

9. The ability to see colors in the auric field may be immediately present in a viewer or may be developed with practice.

10. An easy experiment to give evidence that the aura has mass can be performed with the assistance of a large magnet.

11. A person should be selected to stand near the subject, holding the magnet in his hand. The magnet should be held approximately one and a half to two feet from the subject's body.

12. The subject again takes a deep breath, and the viewers should pay particular attention to the area where the magnet is held. The aura will run to the magnet.

VIEWING YOUR OWN AURA

1. Select a room with a mirror opposite a neutral wall. The bathroom in most houses or apartments works very well for this purpose.

2. Turn off the light in the room being used for the experiment, making sure that a light outside the room emits enough light so that you can distinguish your own features in the mirror.

3. Take a deep breath and imagine the breath filling the head.

4. You should be quickly aware of the aura in the head area.

5. An additional breath may be taken and again directed to the head to increase the intensity of the auric field and make its fluctuations more pronounced.

6. As in viewing the aura of others, your own aura will appear as a light mist or haze.

7. Color discrimination of the aura may be possible immediately or will develop with practice.

EXPERIENCING THE AURA
THROUGH TOUCH

The subject for the exercise should increase the energy in the aura through breath techniques described earlier. Those who take part in the exercise should stand directly in front of the subject, one person at a time, and place their hands approximately six inches from either side of the subject's head. The participant should then close his eyes and allow himself to place all awareness in his hands. The subject then takes another deep breath from the diaphragm and mentally envisions the breath filling and leaving his head.

The participant probably will experience the sensation of heat and the feeling of movement around his hands. This technique has proven very successful in allowing the blind to experience the human aura.

MAGNET EFFECT ON THE AURA

When the subject has placed himself before a neutral wall and raised the level of energy in his aura through breathing, as previously described, the participants place a large horseshoe magnet approximately four inches on either side of the subject's head. Participants will find that placing a magnet in this position while viewing the aura creates an interesting effect. The inner aura will run to or extend to meet the magnet. The magnet can be placed the same distance from the body in any other area, and the same effect will be achieved. This experiment indicates that the aura does possess mass and can be used as a valuable example in answer to the question of afterimagery.

4 Psychokinesis

Of all the areas encompassed by parapsychology, psychokinesis is perhaps the most fascinating and promising area of human potential. Psychokinesis, usually referred to as PK, describes the concept that the mind actually can exert an effect on material objects external to itself. PK has been used experimentally to control the roll of dice and to inhibit growth in cultures of plant diseases. It also has been used to accelerate plant growth and to bring anesthetized mice back to consciousness long before the effects of the anesthetic normally would disappear.

The idea that the mind can traverse space and actually make its effects felt by material objects may at first seem astounding. However, scientists are no longer attempting to prove the possibility of such an occurrence but, instead, are looking for practical applications for a phenomenon already experimentally proven. Research conducted in the Soviet Union by Dr. Pavel Naumov and in the United States by Dr. J. B. Rhine and Dr. Louisa E. Rhine has shown beyond doubt that PK—the ability of the mind to affect material objects—is a reality. Most of the Rhines's subjects did not consider that they could control external events with the sheer force of mind, but most of them showed marked ability in psychokinesis. All subjects evidenced PK ability in varying degrees.

The question of what force or energy is responsible for the PK effect naturally confronts the logical mind. Although no pat answers are available now, several theories have been set forth both in Russia and in the United States.

After studying Mikailova and others trained to develop this latent talent, Soviet scientists proposed the theory that psychokinesis involves the conversion of physical energy into psychic energy, which is then converted to kinetic energy, which leaves the subject and exerts its force on material objects. A major reason for this conclusion is that Mikailova and others lose three to four pounds during an experimental session.

J. B. Rhine has theorized that PK has its basis in the relationship between mind and body. He considers that energy must be used to direct energy; therefore PK begins with the use of direct nervous energy, and nervous energy converts itself to muscular energy. This muscular, or kinetic, energy then directs the movement of material objects. The key to understanding Rhine's approach is to realize that for him the mind is not imprisoned in the physical body but can traverse space and perhaps even time itself.

The important fact to keep in mind is that PK can be studied and measured scientifically. One must also keep in mind that PK is a form of energy that requires considerably more research.

The practical uses to which PK may be put are numerous and varied. A nation that develops in its citizens the ability to deflect the needle of a compass across vast distances in space may gain a strategic weapon. The compass of a ship at sea, the compass of a plane in the air, or the compass of a unit in the field could be deflected by the power of thought alone. Experimentation has shown that PK also can be used to disorient a gyroscope—the mechanism that guides intercontinental ballistic missiles.

Psychokinesis surely will have a marked effect on biology and physics. Biologists traditionally have considered physical effects to be the product of physical causes. PK experiments have shown that it is possible to use the mind to control the rate of the heartbeat—indeed, even to stop the heartbeat—to control the blood pressure, and to impede or accelerate plant growth depending on the will of the person who conveys psychokinetic energy. Biology as a science cannot long ignore experiments that so markedly affect it. Since physics as a science deals with energy, psychokinesis naturally falls in its realm. Physicists well may have to answer the parapsychologist's question: "What is the nature of psychokinetic energy?"

No matter from what discipline comes the answer to this question, the experiments that led to the question cannot and must not be ignored. Discovery of the nature of psychokinesis and laws that govern it may hold the answer to the much talked about energy depletion of the future.

Psychokinesis Exercises

CONTROLLING THE FALL OF DICE

1. Begin by using a pair of dice. After several hours of practice more dice may be added to reduce the number of tosses necessary to obtain statistically significant results.

2. Perform the breath exercises outlined in Chapter 1.

3. It is important to have in your mind a clear picture of the face of the die you want to be uppermost when the dice come to rest.

4. Begin by choosing a number from 1 to 6. For the purpose of illustration we will use the number 3 in discussing this exercise. The dice should be thrown from a cup rather than from the palm of the hand.

5. Keeping the chosen number in mind, take a deep breath, imagine the dice to have already fallen with the desired number on the upturned faces, and throw the dice from the cup. A back-

board should be used and the dice thrown so that they hit and rebound from its surface.

6. With two dice a total of six runs is suggested to ascertain statistical significance above mean chance expectation. Each run should consist of six tosses of the two dice, since the mean chance expectation for any number of tosses is one-sixth of the total dice thrown by chance alone. In 6 runs of 6 tosses each, chance alone would produce 12 hits. Therefore, 17 hits would yield odds of 20 to 1; 18 hits would produce odds of 100 to 1. That is, chance would account for this number of hits only 1 time in 100 trials.

7. The following statistics are given for the use of two dice, six tosses in each trial. In 12 runs mean chance expectation is 24 hits; 30 hits give odds of 20 to 1, and 32 hits odds of 100 to 1.

8. You may reduce the number of runs necessary for statistical significance by tossing six dice simultaneously. In this instance 10 runs, each consisting of 24 tosses, are needed. Since the total number of tosses equals 240, mean chance expectation would be 40 hits or one-sixth of the total number of tosses thrown.

DIVERTING THE NEEDLE ON A COMPASS THROUGH PK

1. The compass need not be expensive but should be one of accepted reliability.

2. Perform the breath exercises described in Chapter 1.

3. Place the compass on a flat surface before you, all other objects in the immediate area removed. Be sure that the compass is placed so that it faces true north and that the needle is not fluctuating.

4. Take another breath. Will the circulation of the breath as previously described. Direct the breath to the fingertips and eyes. Imagine the fingers becoming elongated through the projection of energy leaving through your fingertips. Place the hands above the compass, willing the energy of the breath through the hands as if to actually push the needle in the desired direction by means of the energy extending through the fingers.

5. Visualize this same energy leaving through the eyes. Imagine it as two beams of light that extend from your eyes, make contact with the needle on the compass, and push it in the desired direction.

6. Use your imagination and will to portray in your own mind the actual results you want to achieve. In your own mind see the needle move and accept the fact as already accomplished.

7. Concentrate on the beams of energy leaving your fingers and eyes, pushing the needle in a desired direction of change. You may find it helpful at first to move the hands back and forth above the compass, thereby allowing the energy to gain

momentum as the energy field around the compass itself is disrupted by the PK energy being introduced into it. Most often the needle at first will sway east and west in a small arc, which will increase as you repeat the breathing exercises and the extension of energy to the needle.

8. Once this arc movement is in progress you are ready to begin control of the specific direction the needle will take. For example, if you want the needle to move due east 20 degrees bring both hands above the true north and move them quickly in an eastward direction, allowing the energy from your eyes to push the needle, adding extra momentum to its directional movement.

9. Increasing the degrees of deflection is a matter of practice, and those who seriously want to develop this ability will practice a half-hour each day. Breath exercises, the visualization of energy, and the strength of the will are the key factors in the purposeful use of psychokinetic energy.

MOVEMENT OF SMALL OBJECTS THROUGH PK ENERGY

1. Follow the breathing exercises in Chapter 1.

2. Select a light object, such as a matchstick or paper clip, to begin your practice.

3. Hold the hands above the object as directed in the previous exercise. The object should be cov-

ered with a glass to prevent interference of air currents.

4. Follow the directions given in the previous exercises, choosing the direction in which you want the object to move and directing your energy to impel the object in that direction.

5. Again, serious practice must involve at least a half-hour each day.

5 Mediumship

Of all the areas related to parapsychology, mediumship is the one in which fraudulent practitioners are most frequently found. The validity of mediumship—that is, a discarnate entity, communicating with living beings through a living person called a medium—has been in question since recorded history.

Death itself is an unknown. The question of survival, after death, of the soul or personality can be found in every culture from the cave to the present. The Greek Oracle of Delphi is spoken of historically as a high priestess with the power to act as a bridge between this world and the next. Kings and nation-states consulted her on such matters as battle strategy, weather prediction, and the welfare of departed spirits.

One might consider that man has come a long

way since the time of the Oracle of Delphi, but it is interesting to note that an archaic English law that pronounced all mediums and witches vagrants was not repealed until 1951. The passage of time has done very little to dissuade humans from seeking means of communicating with the dead. The reader may be surprised to discover on investigation that throughout history persons who have led in their fields and have been considered extremely intelligent not only have believed such communication possible but also have attempted to demonstrate its possibility.

Thomas A. Edison was one such pioneer. At 73 Edison was interviewed by the *Scientific American* on his work in the construction of a machine that would allow the living to communicate with the dead. In the October 30, 1920, edition of the *Scientific American* Edison gave his views on the possibilities of life after death and spoke of his work on communication with deceased persons. At about the same time *American Magazine* (October 20, 1920) contained the article, "Edison Working to Communicate with the Next World." Any reader who holds the opinion that to embrace a belief in mediumship shows a lack of intelligence need only ask himself whether the man who invented the phonograph and the alkaline battery could be considered unintelligent.

Emanuel Swedenborg, well-known scientist and philospher in the 17th and 18th centuries, was an enthusiastic supporter of the theory of life after death and of the possibility of communication with the dead. In the late 18th and early 19th centuries such people as Arthur Schopenhauer and Immanuel Kant addressed themselves to the question of soul survival and communication with the next world. Kant, best known for *Critique Of Pure Reason*, published in 1781, also wrote a book little referred to in philosophy classes today. The book, *Dreams of a Ghost Seer*, published in 1776, was concerned mainly with Swedenborg's work in mediumship.

William McDougall wrote *Body and Mind* in 1911. The book was a plea bordering on a demand that science investigate the possible survival of the human personality after death. McDougall taught at Oxford and Harvard and later held a position at Duke University, where in 1927 he engaged Doctors J. B. Rhine and Louisa E. Rhine to set up the parapsychology laboratory to research the psychic field, including mediumship.

The well-known psychologist Carl G. Jung also expounded the belief that the human personality survives bodily death. Jung, whose works are studied today in colleges and universities, reported that he had conversed with discarnate spirits and felt that a particular discarnate acted as his guide in times of stress. Interestingly, Jung's work and beliefs in such areas are rarely, if ever, referred to in psychology classes. How is it possible for this discipline to place such great emphasis on his contributions to psychology and yet completely ignore the time and energy he devoted to parapsychology?

Add to this list of recognized geniuses the name of Socrates, who also conversed with disembodied spirits, and the logical conclusion is that extremely intelligent and creative men have considered communication with the dead possible and have pleaded and demanded that science take an active part in the investigation of soul survival and communication after death.

The average person usually is not aware that mediumship is manifested in many different forms. The most common conception of mediumship, and the form most often used in television and movies, is physical mediumship, which is characterized by the production of such physical phenomena as rushing winds, table levitation, sounds, lights, and general physical disturbances —all reported to be manifestations of disembodied spirits. Of all the forms of mediumship, this one is most open to fraud and trickery. Certainly it would not be difficult for an unscrupulous person to produce such physical phenomena by very ordinary though underhanded methods.

Television and movies also have portrayed direct voice mediumship. In this form the discarnate spirit is supposed to actually speak through the medium so that those present who knew the discarnate before his death are able to recognize the voice of their deceased friend or relative.

A slightly less dramatic form is called mental

mediumship. In this form the medium supposedly sees and hears the deceased spirits and conveys the messages in her own voice but with the recognized speech patterns and idiosyncrasies of the discarnate spirit.

Trumpets announce yet another form, called trumpet mediumship. In this manifestation messages from departed friends and loved ones are announced through a trumpet, which materializes in a mysterious manner and floats about the room in midair while messages are announced to those present. Apparently, though, the flight of the trumpet medium's instrument is aided by very material attached strings.

One of the most interesting forms of mediumship is that in which the medium produces from her body ectoplasm that materializes into a supposed discrete image of the departed individual. It is unfortunate that in such materialization mediumship the medium removes himself from the view of all present and takes up residence in a cabinet! The reason given is that as the ectoplasm leaves the body in such great quantities the physical body becomes withered and extremely grotesque. We know of no scientific experimentation to support such reasoning. Even when psychic experimenters expressed a willingness to risk the gruesome sight, the mediums felt compelled to protect them from foolhardiness by denying them visual access to the cabinet while the séance was in progress.

Whenever a medium finds it necessary to exclude herself from the sitters' visual field, the sitters have reason to become more than a little suspicious. It cannot be stressed too often that any form of mediumship must be seen through open though extremely skeptical eyes. It is far too easy for a bereaved relative or friend to see and hear only what he wants to be the truth; so one must look very carefully, not only at the subject of mediumship but also at the individual medium. This is not to say that all mediums are deliberately fraudulent but only to warn those who would seek out mediums that ethical and nonethical persons exist in every field, including mediumship. Since we have turned our attention to the medium as an individual, let us consider several characteristics that mediums seem to share almost universally.

First, a medium rarely performs effectively in the presence of an antagonistic and closed-minded skeptic. Unfortunately, this characteristic inhibits scientific investigation. Certainly not all scientists are antagonistic or closed-minded, for to consider spending time in such investigation is a mark, hopefully, of some openness on the investigator's part. Add that a very important ingredient in the makeup of any scientist worthy of the name is an open-minded and open-ended approach to any field in which he wants to do research. Nevertheless, investigators and ordinary sitters alike frequently can unwittingly bring prejudice and antagonism into a research situation.

A possible explanation for such disruption in the medium's efficient performance can be found in consideration of vibratory fields and energy patterns. Mediums throughout history have said that work in mediumship requires vast amounts of energy. Whenever extremely negative conditions are present the medium must deploy energy to overcome the negativity before getting down to the business of communication with the next world. Whether this is an adequate explanation is left to the reader; however, except in fraudulent situations, all endeavors require energy. If that energy must be divided, then surely it is possible that energy will be lessened in the performance of the major task at hand.

The second universal characteristic of mediums is that ability to perform fluctuates from month to month, day to day, and even hour to hour. As is true of most abilities, the faculty to perform as a mediumistic channel is not constant, which may explain why some people who possess valid capability to communicate with another world turn to fraudulent practices.

For instance, imagine if you will a medium who has an opportunity to conduct a séance in the presence of people who can be influential in aiding his career. Imagine that in the presence of these people the medium discovers that on this day her ability just happens to have fluctuated on the downside of his effective and impressive performance. What does the medium do? Too often, believing that he is facing a one-time chance, he stoops to fraud, hoping those present will not detect it, and rationalizing in his own mind, "I know I have a real ability, and this may be my only chance to convince these people. I'll cheat now, but never again!"

The medium may be more right than he knows. He may never have the chance again! If an investigator discovers fraud he has no choice but to report the facts as they are, and the facts in such a case can have a long-term damaging effect. The investigator himself may decide that true research in the field is impossible, since it is evident that a person of reputed integrity has compromised himself. The medium, who up until this time may have been completely honest and enjoyed a reputation for openness and integrity, can easily find that all the good that preceded is now washed away like so many soapsuds down a drain.

No matter how the medium rationalizes the fraudulent performance, he will never find an adequate reason for compromising himself and selling out to his own ego. How much more simple would it be if in such circumstances he could just honestly say, "I'm sorry, but for various reasons I cannot operate as a mediumistic channel at this time. I welcome your presence and investigation on another day." The damage that could be prevented by such a simple and open statement is unfathomable. Science needs this type of honesty in mediumship if research is ever to come to sound scientific conclusions.

The last characteristic we shall consider is the medium's inability to use his talents to enhance his own economic status. We refer here not to an economic status that may prosper through client fees but to economic status enhanced by means of investments based on precognitive knowledge direct from the spirit world. Many mediums and psychics believe that the use of precognitive information to enhance one's own financial situation would result in the loss of all ability to attain such information—a belief that has no basis in logic. The true explanation of such a loss of abilities may more likely be found in that an individual obsessed with amassing a fortune may have no time to devote to the continual enrichment of psychic abilities. Precognitive information most generally is obtained in what may be considered an altered state of consciousness, or a state of enriched awareness. One who is preoccupied with materialistic gains probably will spend most of his time out of such states.

The reader's attention is directed now to four theories that attempt to explain the phenomenon of mediumship. Once again the conclusion on which theory accurately explains the mediumistic process must be left to the reader, for much research remains to be done in this area.

The first theory we will consider is that information conveyed through a medium is received telepathically from living beings. This telepathy would be no small feat in itself, but since we are examining the phenomenon of mediumship, telepathic experience would not lend evidence for survival after bodily death.

Perhaps the most interesting point in support of communication with discarnate spirits is that many messages conveyed through mediums are not immediately recognized as valid by those to whom they are conveyed. Research often has borne out the accuracy of a mediumistic message, even though living persons previously associated with the discarnate cannot validate the message.

The second theory is that the medium is able to tap universal mind. This theory has its roots in the ancient belief that there exists a universal ether, known in occult circles as the Akashic records. These records supposedly contain the complete history of a cycle of creation. If such records do, in fact, exist, then a medium or other sensitive possibly could attune himself by altering his state of consciousness to the vibrational level on which these records are kept, and it would be much more difficult to prove through mediumistic methods the existence of life after death.

Carl Jung spoke of the collective unconscious —a state or level of consciousness—in which mankind shares access to vast amounts of information and knowledge. Again it must be stated that much more research must be conducted in order to gain scientific evidence for the existence of universal mind or soul survival. It is important to keep in mind that the existence of a universal intelligence would not necessarily rule out the possibility of communication with discarnate spirits. It would become but one more variable to be seriously considered in mediumistic investigation.

Psychologically, the third theory that attempts to explain mediumship is one of the most interesting yet proposed. The theory states that the medium's messages are a product of his own subconscious mind. This idea, together with the possibility of a splinter personality that the medium is not consciously aware of, creates an intriguing psychological problem. It is quite possible, most likely true, that in many cases this theory can explain mediumistic messages. Psychological journals are replete with studies of split personality. A less frequent occurrence, but one that must be considered, is the multiple personality. Most people are at least acquainted in some way with *The Three Faces of Eve*. Certainly the possibility of a splinter personality in mediumship must be considered.

Physiological tests in combination with psychological testing may prove the researcher's most valuable tool in attempting to determine whether mediumistic conveyances are the product of the medium's subconscious mind. It is enough to say at this time that physiological differences have been substantiated scientifically in the study of several mediums.

Eileen J. Garrett, a world-famous medium and researcher, has allowed open scientific investigation of her mediumistic abilities. Definite physiological changes occurred in Mrs. Garrett's bodily functions when supposed discarnates reportedly were communicating with her. These changes involved wide discrepancies in respiration, pulse rate, electrocardiograph readings, blood count, and blood sugar readings with each discarnate supposedly using Mrs. Garrett as a means of communicating with the living world. Physicians evaluated the findings and determined that no physiological laws now known could explain the wide variations indicated in the laboratory tests, a point that must be considered as fairly heavy evidence on the side of discarnate communication.

The final theory to be considered is that the medium actually becomes a channel through which discarnates communicate information from another world. In evaluating this theory the reader should think again about each of the other theories. If science can rule out all other ways of conveying mediumistic messages, what is left is a strong case in favor of survival after bodily death and a communicative link—the medium—between these two worlds.

To conclude, the reader is asked to remember that truth is not an absolute commodity but is the sum product of intellectual curiosity, an open mind, and a willingness to consider alternative factors. Truth has many different faces, and our perspective of what is true changes as we move to view facts from other vantage points. This is not only the purpose of scientific investigation but is also an obligation of each individual to himself. "Seek and you shall find" can be well applied to formal education and self-education. A closed mind is a dead mind. If we do not move forward we surely disintegrate, because nothing known to science ever remains the same. We must ask questions if we are ever to have answers.

We must investigate mediumship if we are ever to know what is responsible for the phenomenon. The approach to such an investigation advocated here is an open mind and a caution, "Let the sitter beware!"

6   Reincarnation

"You only live once! Or do you?" For centuries man has pondered the question of reincarnation, the doctrine that holds that man lives not one life but many lives on earth. Up to the present day most interest in the doctrine of reincarnation has been confined to the Eastern hemisphere. Only within the last 20 years have scientists in the Western hemisphere seriously researched the question of the human soul's rebirth into another carnal body for the purpose of living out another life not in an afterworld but right here on earth. Even though scientists have only recently begun to study the subject, belief in and investigation of reincarnation has been present for centuries, even in the West.

In considering the theory of reincarnation it is important to understand that we are not concerned here with the theory of transmigration of souls, which holds that souls are reborn on earth in many forms, ranging from trees to lower animals to man. Reincarnation is the rebirth of a soul in another human form only, although the human form itself may change with each incarnation, so that a soul in one lifetime may inhabit the body of a female, and in the next lifetime the body of a male.

The important thing to remember about the theory of reincarnation is that the soul continues to inhabit a human body. However, the theory does allow not only for changes in sex but also for changes in race; that is, a person may incarnate in the yellow race in one lifetime, in the black race in another, the white race or the red race in still other lifetimes. The theory is based on the belief that man must experience everything before he can return to being nothing. This nothing is not a state of bankruptcy but the only state great enough to contain everything.

For centuries Yogis and other mystics have spoken of cycles of creation. In a poetic sense these cycles may be considered days and nights of creation. The Christian Bible, along with the holy books of many religions, holds that all that exists came out of nothing. Eastern religions have expanded on this idea in referring to a day of creation as a state in which the Unmanifest Creator or Absolute becomes manifest. In this process of manifestation the Absolute puts certain limits on itself. All manifest creation knows some limitation; it has a beginning and it has an end. Only in the state of nonmanifestation or nothingness are no limitations to be found.

Once the process of manifestation has begun, the process of centering—the return to the unmanifest state—also has begun. These two processes are different sides of the same coin. Just as there can be no coin with one side, so there can be no beginning of manifestation without the simultaneous beginning of centering—the Absolute pulling everything back to itself—to return to the unmanifest state of nothingness.

So, according to the doctrine of reincarnation, individualized spirit, the soul manifests in the corporeal body of a human being so that it might experience and evolve to the point where it can be brought back to the unit of pure being, nothingness. The words, "the soul is to experience and evolve," form another pillar in the foundation of belief in reincarnation. Those who have taught the doctrine have stated that the soul is evolving along spiritual lines, and with each new lifetime the opportunities needed for its further growth are presented.

This idea of spiritual evolution, or evolution of the noncorporeal soul, is analogous to the idea of physical evolution. We do not intend to speak here for or against the theory of physical evolution but only to point out that a belief in spiritual evolution, or the idea of a growth toward perfection, is not unique to the theory of reincarnation.

A Hermetic teaching states, "As above so below." If man does evolve physically—and certainly biologists, geneticists, and physical anthropologists have produced valid evidence to support this theory—then according to the Hermetic teaching we also can expect the soul to modify itself through experience as it seeks to achieve the state of unity with the Absolute from which it emerged.

But what of Christianity? Do the historical documents of the Christian religion contain any allusions to a doctrine of reincarnation? Let us examine the principle historical document of Christianity, the Bible.

Consider, first, Ecclesiastes 1:9–11: "The thing that hath been, it is that which shall be ... and there is no new thing under the sun. Is there any thing whereof it may be said, See, this is new? It hath been already of old time, which was before us. There is no remembrance of former things." We shall return later to the last sentence in this passage, for it bears greatly on a portion of the foundation for a belief in reincarnation.

The concept that a soul inhabiting one body has previously inhabited the body of a person now deceased is again alluded to in Matthew 11:11–15: "Among them that are born of women there hath not risen a greater than John the Baptist.... For all the prophets and the law prophesied until John: And if ye will receive it, this is Elias, which was for to come. He that hath ears to hear, let him hear." The prophet Elias had long since departed the physical earth; yet by Matthew's word Jesus stated to a multitude that John the Baptist was indeed Elias. Whether we look at the Bible as an inspired book or as a historical document this testimony certainly indicates that those who lived in Christ's time were well acquainted with the idea of reincarnation.

In fact, Christ was thought to be the reincarnation of one of the prophets, as evidenced in Matthrew 16:13–14. "When Jesus came into the coast of Caesarea Philippi, he asked his Disciples, saying, Whom do men say that I the Son of man am? And they said, Some say that thou art John the Baptist: some, Elias; and others, Jeremias, or one of the prophets." This response would have given Christ the perfect opportunity to dismiss as ridiculous the idea that any man could be the reincarnated soul of a man who had previously experienced physical death. Interestingly, the Bible shows no evidence of Christ's repudiating the belief that men who walked the earth in his time could possibly be the reincarnated souls of deceased persons.

Among the many theories about why the doctrine of reincarnation fell out of favor with the Christian church is one that postulates that church and state rulers believed they could more easily control their subjects if the people believed they had a one-time chance to attain heaven. (Keep in mind here that for many centuries church and state were united.) It is in no way suggested here that this is the only possible explanation for the discontinuance of teachings about reincarnation. Possibly few events—most likely no events—have one simple explanation.

Before beginning a discussion of what facts science can offer for and against the theory of reincarnation, let us consider the doctrine of Karma, which is nothing more than the law of cause and effect. The doctrine states simply that by initiating certain actions, man sets into motion laws that carry reactions back to him. Karma does not mean good or bad but simply speaks of reciprocal returns. Many people believe erroneously that if one subscribes to the theory of reincarnation he has license to do anything he wants without fear of denial of heaven or threat of hell. Careful study of the doctrine of karma, though, reveals that, rather than granting license, karma, in fact places on mankind responsibility for every thought and action. The doctrine clearly states that the soul will evolve according to the manner in which it decides to act. Here again the Hermetic teaching of reciprocal returns is reflected in the laws of physics: every action has an equal and opposite reaction.

Karma, as no other world doctrine, places on each individual full responsibility for the exercise of his own free will. According to this doctrine no person can safely rationalize any action or even thought simply by stating, "It wasn't my fault, so-and-so made me do it."

The reader may ask here, "What about circumstances that are not under one's control?" The responsibility still is left with the individual. Although a person may not always control circumstances, the manner in which he responds to such circumstances is completely in the realm of free will and individual choice. A person may feel that the alternatives open are so unsatisfactory as to leave no choice, but the fact remains that no matter how unpleasant alternatives seem they are still alternatives, and one rather than another can be selected. The key here is man's free will. He may try to assuage the pain that ultimate responsibility can bring, but free will marks him indelibly as responsible for even his smallest actions.

Remember that Karma is not concerned with value judgments, or whether a thought or an action is good or bad. Another way to view Karma is to see it as a law of opportunity. If our actions and thoughts are returned to us, then Karma allows each of us the opportunity to freely choose what those returns will be.

In Lloyd C. Douglas's book, *Dr. Hudson's Secret Journal*, Dr. Hudson chooses to receive nonmonetary returns on money loaned to various people. He tells persons who would repay him to keep the money but be obliged to pass it along to someone else if and when they encountered a person in need. He felt that in this way his gift would make a full circle and return to him, perhaps not as money but in some manner that would be beneficial to his life. So the doctrine of Karma has appeared in Western literature even though the word Karma has not been applied to the philosophical thought.

The Christian Bible contains passages that allude to the doctrine of Karma. Perhaps one of the most often quoted passages is Matthew 7:12. "Therefore all things whatsoever ye would that men should do to you, do even so to them: for this is the law and the prophets."

We have mentioned that in reincarnation a soul evolves with each life spent on the earth. The next incarnation of the soul will depend much on what the soul has learned in the previous life. Again we find in the Christian Bible a verse that reflects this belief. In the Apocrypha, The Wisdom of Solomon 8:19–20, we find the words, "Now I was a child good by nature, and a good soul fell to my lot. Nay, rather, being good, I came into a body undefiled."

It is not our purpose here to fully expound the doctrines of reincarnation and Karma; that task would require another book. However, the information given here should acquaint you with these ideas and allow you an opportunity to decide for yourself whether you want to research the doctrines more closely.

Let us now examine the scientific views of

reincarnation. Since intellect and objective evaluation are two of the major tools of scientific investigation, we may begin by asking what events in everyday life suggest the possibility that reincarnation is not merely a theory but an actuality.

One possible way of considering reincarnation is through the discipline of physics. A basic law of physics is the law of conservation of energy, which holds that energy can be neither created nor destroyed but is merely transformed from one state to another. Since all that exists can be reduced to some form of energy, man, too, can be placed in this category. Thomas Edison once stated in his diary, "Life, like matter, is indestructible. There has always been a certain amount of life in this world and there will always be the same amount. You cannot create life; you cannot destroy life; you cannot multiply life." This remark aptly illustrates the first argument in favor of reincarnation.

Another possible argument in support of the validity of the theory of reincarnation has its basis in the self. Evidence found in human nature expresses man's belief in the indestructibility of the personality or ego. Can you think of a time when you did not exist? Do not consider historical events that occurred before your birth but, rather, try to conceive of a state of nonexistence of your own soul or personality. Conceive in your mind, if you can, the point at which you were not!

Small children frequently provide a further illustration of this concept. When adults are discussing occurrences in their childhoods children often ask, "Where was I when you were a child?" It seems impossible for a child to conceive of the time when he did not exist!

Child prodigies suggest another argument in favor of reincarnation. How is it that some children display great talent in certain fields at a very early age? Mozart, for example, was able to play difficult concertos on the piano when he was six years old. Is it possible that a soul which enters life on earth brings with it talents developed in a previous lifetime?

Certainly these are arguments and not conclusive evidence to support the theory of reincarnation. However, they have posed enough questions, to laymen and scientists alike, to initiate research into the phenomenon.

Much of the research has involved regression through hypnosis, a technique that has obvious and subtle drawbacks. First, we do not suggest that everyone interested in reincarnation become engaged in research through hypnotic regression. The use of hypnosis is best left to those clinically or medically qualified. Second, one must consider whether the person who is conducting such experiments has in any way suggested to the subject that he is regressing to a specific time and place. If such suggestions are given even inadvertently, the experimenter may find himself with a beautiful piece of fiction that portrays life in an earlier period. Great care must be taken to give no suggestions that the subject might use as building blocks for the foundation of an imaginary lifetime.

In this type of research more than minimal numbers of problems arise in obtaining specific names and dates. The subject will recall either isolated given names or isolated surnames and is often vague about dates and names of cities or towns. It is easy to understand that the researcher's task in this area is difficult. Many times when specific names and dates are given they refer to a time prior to recorded history, which makes verification all but impossible.

The investigator's work into reincarnation is not always aided when specific names and dates given lie within the range of written history. Then the researcher must rule out any possibility that the subject may have come on the information while reading, attending a movie, listening to a conversation, or engaging in some academic study that would have covered the area mentioned. However, careful research into the history of the time may strongly suggest the validity of the subject's statements. For example, a subject may recount a life in which he was an ordinary citizen, with no claims to fame. If the subject also gives dates and facts about this earlier person's life, and his account is proved valid through close research, the investigator may consider that he has a case suggestive of reincarnation.

In several universities scientists well qualified in the fields of medicine, psychology, and physics are conducting research along these lines. Another line of research simultaneously taking place attempts to explain verified information suggestive of reincarnation by means of the theory of genetic memory. Scientists who are investigating the possibility that man is born into this life with racial memories are considering the possibility that our genes convey to our children not only biological but also memory characterisitics.

Flatworms have been used in several studies to test this hypothesis. A generation of flatworms trained to prefer light rather than dark spaces is killed after evidence of learning has been shown, and a food product is prepared from the remains. This food stuff then is fed to a group of flatworms not trained to prefer lighted areas. The offspring of this group, with no previous training, have selected lighted rather than dark areas. This experiment to explore the possibility of genetic memory, however, is no more conclusive at this time than are thoroughly researched cases suggestive of reincarnation. To arrive at a perspective of truth one must see clearly from many different vantage points. The scientist must always be the objective viewer, systematically researching various possibilities until the best possible explanation is reached in the process being investigated.

If the reader has access to small children he can conduct his own research. Small children often refer to events that would necessarily have had to occur in a former life if they occurred at all.

Several students at Georgia State University have related experiences along these lines with their own children.

One such incident is the case of a student's five-year-old daughter who refused to ride in an airplane. The child told her mother that she wanted never to ride in an airplane because previously she had been killed in an airplane crash. The child was quite emphatic in stating that before her present life she had died in a fiery plane crash. Further, the child said this crash occurred when she was grown up, not a little girl. The child's mother was disturbed by the story and feared the youngster might be experiencing a clairvoyant impression of her own future. Although such an impression is possible in the light of many similar recorded cases it does not seem probable.

Other cases involving such reports from youngsters include a six-year-old's tale of a life as a seaman on a sailing ship, with a vivid description of sailing vessels and a sketchy but impressive account of navigation. Another child who claimed to have died of a specific disease recounted symptoms that were medically verified as those that would accompany the illness.

If the reader finds an opportunity he can take advantage of the chance for research by writing down the facts the child relates. He should question the child in an attempt to gain more specific information, but he must be very careful at all times not to suggest anything to the child that

73

could feed the youngster's imagination. With such facts in hand the student might research the material at a good reference library, and if the facts involve a foreign country he might contact agents in that country who could verify or deny the facts.

When the subject of reincarnation is being considered, students of parapsychology at Georgia State University most often question earth's increasing population. Where do all the new souls come from?

A tenet of reincarnation holds that the soul when sufficiently evolved may choose not only the time in which it wants to incarnate but also the specific circumstances into which it will be introduced. Therefore, many souls may delay the beginning of another life on earth until the conditions necessary to their own personal experience are present. Even though this idea often surprises students, since it places on them the responsibility for having chosen their life circumstances, they are willing to consider it as a possible explanation for population growth.

We will not deal with astrology here but do want to point out that astrology as a science has much evidence to support its validity. If a soul can choose its moment of incarnation, then according to the science of astrology the time that contains an exact set of circumstances for any individual comes around every 25,000 years. That is, if an astrologer were to cast the natal chart of an individual 25,000 years would pass before that individual would find exactly the same astrological conditions.

If the reader feels any reluctance to consider astrological information he should be aware that Carl Jung strongly believed that the astrological moment of birth stamped the individual with an indelible mark or tendency toward encountering certain circumstances. Remember, as before, that man's free will in regard to response to these circumstances is always an intervening factor.

Where the soul resides and what it does between incarnations is a question science cannot attempt to answer at this time. Yoga and other mystical religions teach that the soul spends this time in another dimension or plane of existence. They propose the existence of many such dimensions or planes, which the soul inhabits according to its level of spiritual evolvement. These religions teach that during its habitation of these planes the soul's function is to consider mistakes made and experience gained in previous lifetimes, and that the soul will decide what new experience it wants in its next incarnation as well as what experiences will best stimulate and enhance its spiritual evolvement. As previously stated, no scientific proof is available for the existence of such way stations between incarnations, nor is there proof positive that reincarnation is a fact.

It is encouraging to realize that scientists are contributing increasing amounts of time and energy to research in all fields encompassed by parapsychology, including reincarnation. It is not for science to judge whether reincarnation is indeed a fact. The purpose of scientific investigation is to research possibilities and present the evidence to be evaluated in regard to any topic, whether that evidence supports or disproves the theory being investigated.

Perhaps it is a mark of intellectual evolvement and a new openness of the mind that scientists are trying to answer questions that only a decade ago they would not even acknowledge. We can only hope the spirit of openness that has allowed inroads in fields that promise great benefit and knowledge to mankind is but a beginning—the vanguard announcing a new renaissance of human potential.

7   Dermaoptics

The literal definition of dermaoptics is skin sight, but this explanation of the phenomenon is inadequate. By means of dermaoptics a sighted person can learn to read through sealed opaque envelopes and discern the contents of photographs or written material enclosed in them. The phenomenon also allows an individual to discern color through touch without actually seeing the color with the eyes.

Although these acts may sound astounding, they have indeed occurred. For two years research and classes have been conducted at Georgia State University, where the techniques were first introduced and refined. Students in a psychology course offered through the School of Special Studies at Georgia State University not only learned rather quickly to distinguish the content of photographs sealed in envelopes but also were able to report both tactile and emotional sensations that reflected the situation portrayed in the pictures.

Historically, the concept of dermaoptics is not new. At conferences on psychology persons reported to have this ability have been introduced. The Russians also have conducted research with individuals able to display the phenomenon. One of the chief differences between dermaoptics as discussed here and as historically discussed is that previously it was thought to be a unique gift that only a few individuals possessed. It will become clear on reading this chapter that dermaoptics is not limited to a gifted elite but is an ability contained in human nature itself.

The ability, in fact, lies dormant in most of the world's population. Classes and research conducted with a cross-section of the population have shown beyond doubt that with adequate training and the use of the proper techniques the ability can be placed literally at the fingertips of any individual interested enough to receive instruction.

Dermaoptics offers much to mankind, but offers even more to those who, either having been born blind or having lost their sight after birth, are without eyesight. We shall treat the sighted and the unsighted separately in relation to dermaoptics, since the techniques involved in putting each group in touch with this innate ability are somewhat different.

First we shall consider dermaoptics as it af-
fects both the congenitally blind and those who
through some trauma or disease became blind after
birth. To teach a person born blind to distinguish
color is a matter entirely different from teaching a
person who at least has some concept of the
meaning of the word color. This difference becomes clear in working with students who have
become sightless in their early teens or late twen-
ties compared with students who were born blind.

The unique difficulties involved in attempting to teach color distinction may become
clearer if one keeps in one's own mind what images the word color brings to him, and then considers the individual with no concept of what the
term connotes. It would be impossible to ask such
a person what color he feels has been placed in his
hands without first explaining to him what a
sighted person means by color. Add to this basic
obstacle the complexity of various tones and
shades in just one color; for example, the student
must learn not merely to distinguish blue from
red, but to distinguish light blue from dark blue,
royal blue from navy blue, and all the gradations
in between. This learning process is no small task
for either instructor or student. Patience and a fa-
cility to communicate ideas are the bedrocks on
which instruction must ultimately rest.

We do not intend here to teach people how to
instruct the blind in such techniques. As was mentioned previously, instruction in dermaoptics for

those without the gift of eyesight must take its own unique path. However, it is important to point out some of the results obtained in using variations of dermaoptics.

One case of a young man born blind, a student we shall call Johnny, typifies other such cases. Johnny requested instruction in the techniques of dermaoptics after speaking with a close friend, also blind, who had been taught these methods. The friend had learned not only how to distinguish colors through touch but also how to discern the content of photographs and slides projected on a wall as well as the content of everyday printed matter—all through dermaoptics. Johnny's friend had one advantage: he had lost his sight at age 13 and could remember how colors looked. He also understood the concept of various shades of the same color.

After speaking with Johnny, who at this time was 18 years old, and explaining to him that most likely no two sighted people see a color in exactly the same way, instruction and training began. Johnny was told that what the sighted world knows as color is actually made up of fields of energy that give off vibrations unique to each individual color; so he had to recognize a certain combination of vibrations, label it with the color name humans had decided to give it, and be able to recall that label when he felt the same vibrations in the future. In this way Johnny learned to distinguish one color from another and apply the proper name to it, and he also was able to describe the content of photographs by using variations of the same technique. A new world has opened for Johnny, a world of which his mind could not previously conceive. Without the gift of eyesight the dimension of color has come to have meaning and importance in his life.

Johnny's friend Bill experienced a gradual loss of sight until he became totally blind at 13. Bill was anxious to learn the techniques for bringing color back into his world and had some very good reasons for wanting to work as hard as necessary in order to accomplish this feat. Most sighted people probably never would have considered many of the reasons that motivated this young man. In conversations he spoke of a desire to be able to match his clothes so that colors went well together, and to see photographs in family albums and to spend some of his leisure time looking at pictures in magazines. Bill worked harder than any other student, blind or sighted, that I have taught. Now he is able to distinguish colors, describe the content of photographs, and place his hands on or above a magazine article, letter, or book in ordinary print and comprehend the theme of the written material.

To date, no student trained through these techniques can discern word-by-word content of ordinary printed material; but research continues, and possibly some day such content reading will be an actuality for the blind. However, for a person without eyesight to be able to discern the themes of articles in everyday magazines is not inconsequential. The implications these results hold for the many thousands of people without sight are tremendous. A human being previously regarded as handicapped becomes a functioning part of society!

Bill is a perfect example of how development of these innate abilities can change a life. Totally blind, he is now employed in a national firm where a major part of his job entails work with blueprints. Bill deserves much credit as an individual. His progress is a hopeful sign to countless other blind students who can now find new sight, not through their eyes, but through the techniques of dermaoptics and extended sensory perception.

The reader may ask, "How are such things possible?" Our theory is that a person can learn to perceive color, sound, taste, fragrance, and touch by extending the normally accepted limits of the five senses. We further hold that since all things, including color and printed material, ultimately are composed of energy in one form or another, by extending the senses one can learn to perceive and interpret the vibrational fields that various energy patterns project. To further explain this position we theorize that although humans have divided perception and allocated it, one form of perception to one perceptor, the human body actually is itself a sensing mechanism with power to receive and interpret all perceptions through any area of its surface. That is, it is possible not only to perceive tactile sensations through the skin but also to learn to hear, smell, see, and taste with any area of the skin surface.

The components of this theory are extremely important, for by making these assumptions it becomes feasible to teach dermaoptics. In learning to tap this ability, just as in learning to tap telepathic ability, the more one brings the senses into play, the easier it seems to develop the faculty.

To clarify this point let us consider how a person can learn to distinguish, through touch alone, the colors red and blue. By extending the senses beyond normally accepted limitations the individual quickly becomes aware that color consists of qualities he may never have considered. Until he familiarizes himself with these other qualities of color no attempt is made to enclose the colored material in order to remove it from his line of vision. (Remember here that we are dealing now with instructions in dermaoptics for sighted people.) Care is taken that the same material, composition, and size is used in each exercise, thereby ruling out the possibility that a person might be making a distinction not by extending his senses but by perceiving a difference in size of the two pieces of colored construction paper.

Let us begin with the color red. Consider the possibility that the color red, or redness, has several unique qualities that no other color possesses. After performing the breath exercises described in

Chapter 1 close your eyes and be aware of the feeling of temperature connected with the color red. Is there warmth or lack of warmth? Next, to extend your sense of hearing and be aware of the sound of redness, which may seem strange at first. You will soon learn, though, that a definite and unique sound is inherent in redness itself.

Attention is turned next to the sense of taste. While holding the red construction paper between your hands extend the sense of taste into the color red and allow yourself to become aware of the taste of redness. In using the olfactory sense, next the reader is asked to become aware only of the fragrance of redness. Texture is considered next— not the texture of the paper, or any particular material, but the texture of redness itself. Does the student experience redness as smooth, rough, soft, or hard? Does the color red carry with it a sensation of movement or rest? What emotional feelings are stimulated through the total perception of redness? All these factors must be considered, experienced, and assimilated.

The reader is asked to follow exactly the same procedure with a sheet of blue construction paper of the same size. After experiencing each of the sensations mentioned for red, touch first the red piece of paper and then the blue in order to experience the same quality as uniquely expressed by each color. Perform this exercise until you can recognize the unique tastes, sounds, textures, and fragrances of red and blue simply by placing your hands on or above any material of these two colors.

Using this same method, by means of practice and recall you may enlarge your capacity for distinguishing colors and various shades of the same color. When an individual has become proficient in recognizing the unique qualities of both the primary and secondary colors through touch alone, he is ready to move to the next step, in which the sighted person is taught to perceive pictures and written material sealed in opaque envelopes. Here, in addition to perceiving color, one learns to distinguish inanimate from animate objects, outdoor scenes from indoor photographs, and emotional states portrayed in the photographs. For written material the student is taught to comprehend an article or a poem enclosed in the same type of envelope.

Various techniques allow the student to distinguish human beings from animals and plants and, further, to identify specific species of animals. For example, to recognize that an animal is in the photograph and to know that it is a rabbit and not an elephant involves variations in techniques designed to allow the person to expand his senses of touch and hearing.

In learning to sense inanimate objects a person may receive a sealed opaque envelope that contains a photograph of a kitchen. One is taught to recognize such details as the presence of flowers in a centerpiece, the pattern in the curtains, whether the floor is carpeted or tiled, and the visible presence of cooking utensils and any visible foods, as well as to identify the colors in the photograph.

When photographs contain outdoor scenes, such as a photograph of Maine's rocky coastline, students are able to identify the presence of, say, the ocean, using their senses of hearing, touching, tasting, and smelling. By extending his ordinarily accepted five senses the student is able to perceive, experience, and interpret the presence of sand and jagged rocks.

As was stated, one of the most beautiful promises this technique holds for the sighted person is the ability to experience conditions reflected in the photograph itself. Thus one can not only look at a picture of a thunderstorm but also feel the rain and wind, smell the freshness of the air, hear the thunder, and see the lighting. This form of total perception makes it possible to experience a situation as a camera or an artist's brush captures it instead of merely looking at a picture and trying to imagine the conditions reflected on a canvas or roll of film.

One might well imagine the implications these techniques hold for education. In addition to offering creative educational methods for thousands of blind students, they bring an entirely different perspective to the business world in that the blind possibly could be employed in many businesses and professions that have been closed to them. The educator will have to reorient his teaching methods to prepare blind students for the increase in possible job opportunities. Blindness will necessarily be viewed as less limiting, and a new approach that concentrates on a student's potential will replace the old view of education for the blind. This educational approach will not be limited by a world view that has seen the loss of eyesight as an irrevocable handicap.

Educators who use these techniques will have the opportunity to make experience important in the educational process. A teacher will be able to have his class experience hot, arrid deserts or cool, moist lowlands rather than merely conveying descriptions and assigning readings.

The comprehension of written material by means of these techniques promises a new method in teaching students with learning disabilities and reading problems. It also offers new hope to adults who for one reason or another left school with inadequate or poor reading skills. As with any technique, reading comprehension through these methods is not a panacea, but surely this form of instruction opens new pathways in education.

In the comprehension of everyday printed material the possibility that a person may be able to learn word-by-word content reading through this method has been considered and is now being researched. Results so far have revealed an interesting problem that is related to the need, in the beginning, to teach students to expand all areas of awareness. In order to achieve content reading by this method it becomes necessary to narrow the field of expanded awareness by degrees. This delicate balance, involving expansion and contraction of the perceptual field, requires much time in achievement. Small successes have to this time been encouraging and have pointed the way toward modification of the methods to allow for greater accuracy in perceiving content verbatim. At the present time students are able to identify correctly several key words in a sentence, but the technique for constricting the field of expanded perception has not been sufficiently perfected to allow for an exact reading of the order of words in a sentence. Presently, though the student may be able to pick out key words, the sequence in which they are perceived is seldom accurate.

Several major thoughts should be considered before we conclude this discussion of dermaoptics. Think for a moment about your own ideas and feelings about blindness. Before the world's population views blindness from a perspective of what is possible for the blind person rather than seeing only his limitations, a change must occur in the way people view blindness. Before our educational system puts into practice creative techniques for dealing with those our society labels handicapped, society must understand that with the proper instruction these people have much to offer to it. You are such a person, and a member of society. Think about the possibilities these techniques offer in the area of human resources and evaluate them in your own mind.

Someone once said that democracy is not the perfect form of government, but it is the best we have so far. These techniques are not cure alls, but they offer more promise than any of the methods previously available. We sincerely hope that further research and implementation of the techniques will bring this promise to fulfillment, but before that happens each individual must allow himself to see the benefits such techniques can bring to our society and to our world.

Progress is made when man can see the possibilities in further investigation into a field; that is, when man *allows* himself to see. Many people in this nation are sightless and are labeled blind. A wise man once said, "There are none so blind as those who will not see."

Exercises for Dermaoptics

PERCEIVING WORDS IN A SEALED ENVELOPE.

1. Each person who participates in this exercise writes three unrelated words in English on a piece of paper. For beginners the words should be either nouns or verbs. The words should be written in pencil when subjects are first learning the technique, since for some reason vibratory energy seems to be more easily interpreted in written form when placed on the paper by means of a soft lead pencil. As one progresses any plain printed material will be read easily.

2. The papers are placed in opaque envelopes and sealed. The envelopes should be exchanged so that no participant holds his own.

3. Hold the envelope between the palms of the hands and perform the breath exercises outlined in Chapter 1.

4. Now unfocus your eyes, a task most easily accomplished by staring downward and inward

toward the nose. Unfocusing the eyes will aid in setting the conscious mind aside.

5. While holding the envelope between the palms of the hands and with the eyes out of focus, allow yourself to be aware of any words, pictures, or emotional sensations you experience. It is extremely important that impressions not be censored but written immediately on a separate sheet of paper while holding the envelope in one hand.

6. The impressions gained in this manner are free flow impressions, and spontaneity cannot be overemphasized.

7. After writing down a minimum of six impressions open the envelope and compare your impressions with the words taken from the envelope.

8. You may notice that when you do not pick up exactly the same words as those sealed in the envelope you will have picked up words closely associated with the sealed words. This phenomenon is very common and is similar to the technique used in artillery practice when a target is ultimately hit by zeroing in from both sides. For example, if the words on the paper in your envelope were sun, apple, and flight, you may have written your impressions as bright, warm, fruit, movement, running, and apple. Apple would, of course, be a direct hit. Bright and warm are closely associated with the word sun, and fruit also would be considered as closely associated with apple. The words *movement* and *running* can be directly

associated with flight. Only through practice will you become proficient in this technique and move from associative words to direct hits.

PERCEIVING A PHOTOGRAPH IN A SEALED ENVELOPE

1. A nonparticipant should select photographs to be used. Place the photographs in opaque envelopes and seal them. So that each participant has the opportunity to give his impressions of the contents of each envelope, the envelopes should be numbered sequentially. Five such photographs should be used in learning this technique. The number, of course, may be enlarged, but each participant should have the experience of interpreting the contents of at least five envelopes.

2. Hold the envelope between the palms of the hands. Breath exercises should be followed as previously outlined, but with one variation. Imagine or will the breath exhaled through your hands. This method allows for increased awareness through the palms. The ancients taught, and research seems to bear them out, that consciousness follows the breath.

3. Place your eyes out of focus as instructed in the previous exercise and again allow free flow of impressions to enter your awareness. Again you are cautioned to write your impressions exactly as received. If one begins to censor or question impressions, the conscious mind is brought into ac-

tion, and extrasensory perception does not operate on the level of the conscious mind.

4. After having written free flow impressions you may question your higher awareness by seeking more specific information about free flow impressions. For example, if during this period of free flow impressions you have received the energy pattern of an animal, you may receive more specific information by extending your senses to discern whether the animal has fur or a tough skin. This form of questioning, the higher awareness, allows great accuracy in interpretation. Allow one minute for each envelope.

5. After one minute the envelopes should be exchanged and the same procedure followed with the next photograph. Continue until each participant has written his impressions for five different envelopes; note the number of each envelope next to the impressions received from it.

6. The nonparticipant now may collect the envelopes and open them sequentially. For example, the envelope marked 1 should be opened and the photograph held so that each participant can see what the picture depicts and check correct impressions.

7. You will find that your accuracy greatly increases as you continue to practice this technique.

8 Meditation

Meditation has become a frequently used word in our society, even among children. It is doubtful that all who use the word are fully aware of its meaning, and if the meaning is clear to them probably the process of entering a meditative state is not at all clear.

Yogis have discussed meditation for centuries, but not until recent times has the Western world turned its attention to this practice. Perhaps the delay stems from cultural differences between East and West. People raised in a Western culture are taught to value actions and overt accomplishments. Probably each reader at one time in his life has come across or heard the expressions: "An idle mind is the devil's workshop"; "Busy hands are happy hands"; "Keeping busy is the best way to stay out of trouble." These expressions reflect an orientation in Western society away from passive states and toward action.

An examination of Eastern societies—India, for example—reveals an orientation not toward outward activity but more toward inner reflection and passive acceptance. Many stories are told of Yogis who have sat under trees and meditated so long that the roots of the trees have grown around them. Since human beings often tend to exaggerate, this story probably does not actually reflect facts, but it indicates the value system of a nation oriented toward introspection and passive states of awareness.

It would be difficult to imagine a Western businessman spending so much time in meditation under a tree. Ours is an industrial nation, and the activity that keeps its wheels in motion is essential to its survival. Perhaps, as in most extremes, a philosophy that lies between these two orientations and incorporates the best premises of each will allow individuals very much in touch with themselves to live in prosperous nations.

Perhaps Western civilization has taken so long to consider the benefits to be derived through meditative states because until very recently the West has viewed meditation as a religious practice, engaged in by persons who had committed their lives to monasteries or convents. Monks, abbots, priests, and nuns came to mind when meditation was mentioned. Today, after many radical changes in the religious orders, meditation has moved outside religion. Businessmen, housewives, high school and college students are reading books and taking courses in the practice of meditation. Certainly not all or even most of these people want to learn meditation in order to reach the state of samadi, the state of perfect attunement with the universe and the Absolute. People are becoming aware that in addition to its use in attaining such a state of awareness, the practice of meditation affords many side benefits, not the least of which is a state of calmness. Consider the millions of dollars spent for tranquilizers each year in this country alone, and it becomes clear that a feeling of tranquility is greatly sought after. Meditation affords a natural means of attaining inner peace together with a major reduction in drug bills.

In order to answer the question "What is meditation?" we will consider first some of the Yoga teachings. A Yogi meditates in order to reach a state of unity with creation and the Creator. Meditation for the Yogi is a process directed at the attainment of unity through a stilling of the conscious mind, thereby expanding awareness. This process affords the individual an opportunity to experience higher states of consciousness and ultimately a state of pure beingness. Yogis do not meditate in order to activate clairvoyant, telepathic, and other abilities usually thought of as extrasensory perception. These abilities are under the conscious control of many Yogis, but such control is not the aim of their meditation.

For the Yogi one means of facilitating the attainment of unity is to awaken the chakras—points where energy can flow from one body to another. Yogis believe that the human is made up of inter-penetrating bodies, each an exact duplicate of the other and each composed of energy moving at various rates of speed in relation to the movement of molecules in the human body. This belief needs no detailed discussion here; the reader need only understand that for the Yogi meditation entails stimulation of these chakras by oxygen circulated through the bodies. The seven chakras range from the base of the spine to the top of the head; thus Yogis believe that meditation should be practiced with the spine straight and erect.

Sound has been used for centuries to induce a state of higher attunement. Mantras, collections of words that when chanted produce specific sounds, have been used extensively to put the conscious mind aside and elevate the awareness to full unity. Mantras are still used today and are being used in the Western hemisphere. Yogis conceive of the word om as being the cosmic sound, and it is often chanted vocally and mentally while entering a meditative state.

Meditation mantras have been used in many different societies. The American Indian used a form of meditation mantras and sacred dances to achieve higher states of awareness. Man through the centuries apparently has believed in the power of words and sound to bring about changes in the material world. The Roman Catholic church has made extensive use of Gregorian chant, and chanting very frequently precedes meditation in religious orders. St. Augustine once said in reference to the use of chants, "To sing is to pray twice."

A second answer to the question of what meditation is comes from the scientist. Even though it has taken many thousands of years for science to attempt an answer, much research has been conducted and is continuing today in many universities and colleges.

A study of brain waves emitted during a meditative state has shown that cerebral activity in such a state is markedly different from activity during routine existence. By means of the electroencephalograph (EEG) it has been determined that during meditation the brain emits a rather constant flow of alpha rhythms. As the meditative state deepens, the EEG reflects the emission of theta rhythms. Both of these states are indicative of less cortical activity and an increase in serenity, and have been found to correlate in a positive manner with states conducive to creativity.

The reader must be careful not to confuse these states with that brought about by sleep. It has been shown through research on the brain's activity during various levels of sleep that when one is sleeping on a very deep level the brain emits delta rhythms. All these rhythms of the brain, as reflected by the EEG, differ from the brain waves emitted while engaging in everyday activity, when beta rhythms are most commonly emitted.

Science has also found it possible to train

people to produce alpha and theta rhythms at will. Such teaching methods always involve the use of an EEG or biofeedback equipment, because only with the use of such equipment can one know with certainty that he is producing alpha or theta rhythms. The reader should keep this point in mind if he ever considers a course of study that claims instruction in the production of brain waves. Without the use of biofeedback there is no sure way of knowing that one is producing alpha rhythms or theta rhythms.

Laboratory tests conducted on blood samples taken from persons before, during, and after meditation show that the lactate level in the blood decreases during the meditative state. This physiological measure indicates a decrease in anxiety level and is a sign of greater calmness. It has also been found that blood pressure is lowered during a meditative state, with a corresponding retardation of the heartbeat.

Unquestionably the meditative state does produce measurable changes in the human body. The direction of change indicates that meditation is instrumental in bringing about creative states, heightened perceptual awareness, and a feeling of serenity within the individual. Thus the production of meditative states may offer much in the field of psychotherapy. The psychotherapist may aid his patients by instructing them in the practice of meditation. Large numbers of psychotherapists have claimed that anxiety is one of the chief problems for therapy. If the therapist can provide his patient with a relatively quick means of relieving anxiety feelings, therapy sessions certainly will be more productive, and the patient will find that this new feeling of serenity has a positive effect on his everyday life.

Psychotherapy may benefit through many of the areas of parapsychology. Clairvoyance and telepathy may enable the therapist to gain greater insights into his patients' problems, and meditation offers the patient the possibility of early relief of anxiety. Research in this area is needed to discover the means by which parapsychology can best aid the therapist. Then patients could benefit from the newly opened avenues of heightened self-awareness that lead to greater fulfillment of human potential. The research being conducted now in Atlanta, Georgia, has not yet produced conclusive findings, but indications are that new inroads will be made in the field of psychotherapy using parapsychological techniques.

Though many people may believe that the better way is to continue the search for breakthroughs in what they may consider more conventional areas, we cannot help but feel that parapsychology will open many doors previously closed to the researcher. We are reminded of the Zen story of the man who clings to the window bars when the door behind him is open! An open door invites scientists and others to pass through toward the light beyond and discover new techniques for tapping and enriching human potential.

Meditation Exercises

There are many techniques for entering a meditative state. Here are several methods for the reader's consideration. No single technique described will work well for every person; so it is very important that one try different meditation methods and remain with the one he finds most beneficial in the practice of meditation.

CIRCULATION OF THE BREATH

1. Most important is the proper meditation posture. You may want to meditate lying down or seated in a chair, but in either case the position chosen should be comfortable and the spine should be kept straight.

2. Choose a chair with a back high enough to support the head. Place the feet flat on the floor and keep the arms uncrossed. The palms of the hands should be left in an upturned position with the backs of the hands resting on the thighs.

3. Close your eyes and pay particular attention to your breathing but make no effort to control

the breath. As you watch the breath you will find that the breathing process will be naturally slowed and deepened.

4. Since according to occult teachings, the breath enters the body and travels downward along the spine, make a conscious effort to control the breath and recirculate it so as to carry it back up the spine and into the area of the pineal gland (to the occult, the third eye).

5. In order to control the breathing and recirculate the breath in this manner, after watching the breathing process without interference, become aware of the breath's deepening and slowing and begin conscious control.

6. Control of the breath must never become a contest of endurance. Suggested measured counts for inhalation, hold and circulation, and exhalation are given here with a caution to begin with a number comfortable for you and increase the count as you progress naturally. All breathing should be from the diaphragm so that on inhalation the diaphragm and abdomen become slightly extended.

7. Begin by inhaling to a measured count of three; relax the stomach muscles immediately when the inhalation is complete. Visualize the breath's traveling down the spinal column, turning, and recirculating up the spinal canal to the pineal gland just above and between the eyebrows. This circulation should be visualized to the measured mental count of six.

8. After circulation of the breath, exhale through the nostrils to a measured count of three. This process of inhalation, hold, circulation, and exhalation should be performed four times.

9. Then simply allow yourself to become aware of your own consciousness and follow the pattern of thoughts that enter into your awareness.

10. This exercise in meditative awareness should continue for no longer than 15 or 20 minutes. This time period is also suggested for the various techniques that follow. As you become more practiced in meditation you may want to extend your meditation to two sessions per day. Then early morning and early evening are suggested.

11. For this meditative technique, as for all that follow, attempt to choose one particular location, which should be as free from noise as possible. The telephone should be adjusted so as to avoid an interruption by an unexpected call. If possible, meditate at a previously arranged time and become accustomed to having this period set aside for meditation. We do not mean to imply that your life should revolve around your meditation schedule but only that you should adhere to a specified time as often as is reasonably possible.

PROJECTION TOWARD THE LIGHT

1. This technique, as all methods enumerated here, may be used either seated or in a prone position. For illustration we shall use the prone position.

2. Lie flat on your back and perform the breathing technique outlined in the first exercise.

3. With the eyes closed visualize a pinpoint of light outside yourself, just in front of the third eye.

4. Be conscious only of the pinpoint of light and will your awareness to move toward and into this light.

5. If any thought of the day enters your awareness you should set the thought aside and continue conscious projection toward and into the light.

6. Allow awareness only of the light and beingness while consciously projecting, always deeper, into its composition.

7. This technique is extremely good for the experience of pure existence. It has an intense calming effect that will remain with you long after the meditation exercise has been completed.

COLOR MEDITATION

1. After performing the breath exercises outlined in the first exercise, select a color. Blue is suggested. Visualize a field of dark blue light outside yourself and just above the third eye region.

2. Consciously project yourself into the color blue, experiencing as you do the qualities of blueness.

3. Keep the awareness focused on blueness itself, and give particular attention to the sound,

fragrance, taste, and texture associated with the color.

4. Allow your awareness to become permeated by these qualities. Blue has a particularly calming effect and is a great aid in expanding philosophical awareness.

5. Again, all thoughts concerned with daily activities should be set aside. The consciousness should be brought back to the experience of the innate qualities of the color blue.

6. Other colors may be chosen. For the particular qualities associated with colors, refer to Chapter 3, "Human Aura," where the significance of colors was discussed.

THE PROJECTION SCREEN TECHNIQUE

1. Perform the exercise for circulation of breath.

2. Visualize a pure white projection screen outside yourself and, again, before and above the third eye area.

3. Keep all awareness focused on this screen, and allow your awareness to follow the flow of any thoughts, forms, sensations, or pictures that play on the screen.

4. Whenever a scene is projected across this mental screen visualize and project yourself into and through the outward appearance of such a

scene. This will allow you to experience the inner qualities associated with form, color, and thought.

5. Problem-solving by this technique may be accomplished by visualizing the projection screen, mentally stating the problem to which you are seeking a solution, and placing all your awareness on the screen. The pictures that play across the screen often will portray the solution.

6. Keep in mind that you must always project yourself through whatever plays across the screen, for meditation implies a deepening awareness and a constant penetration into whatever appearances occur.

SOUND MEDITATION THROUGH MUSIC

1. Select classical or semiclassical recorded music that appeals to you. The theme from 2001 ("Also Sprach Zarathustra") is suggested as an appropriate musical score for the practice of meditation with sound.

2. As the music begins, lie flat on your back, close your eyes, and watch your breath but make no attempt to control it. Watch the breath in this manner for approximately 30 seconds; then turn your full awareness to the music.

3. Project yourself into each note and be carried up and down the musical scale so that your

consciousness becomes entwined with the melody itself.

4. If possible, position your body in such a way that vibrations that fill the room can be felt physically. This sensation can be an aid in allowing your consciousness to become the music.

5. Like the music, allow your consciousness to fill all space. Flow with it into every corner of the room. With the vibrations of music penetrate the walls of the room, and project yourself as music into infinite space. You may be surprised, particularly with the Zarathustra theme, to find yourself experiencing creation itself and penetrating through creation to whatever force has set it in motion.

6. Continue this meditation for at least one minute after the music has stopped. You will find that a calm state of exhilaration and expanded awareness will remain with you long after the exercise.

Practice each of these techniques for one week before deciding which method offers you the greatest benefit in meditation. You may find a combination of techniques most profitable. Whatever works best for you is for you the best method of meditation.

With practice you may develop variations of several techniques. Variations are encouraged if they aid entrance into a meditative state of unity with all that is!

9 Visualization

Many books have been written on the subject of positive mental attitude and the effect it can have in everyday living. We shall not attempt here to encourage a Pollyanna outlook on life but shall state some basic facts and a hypothesis that suggests that man is the creator of his own future. We are not speaking here of the past built day on day, one event leading to another. Right now, in fact, the reader possesses the ability to bring into his life future circumstances and events by mentally creating those events today! This may seem astounding, but as one reads on it will become clear to him that he has more control over his future than he ever dreamed.

Since time is not an absolute commodity but a flowing continuum, man has the ability to project his thoughts into what at this time he considers the future and to form it in the pattern he desires. The basis for this ability is that all things, including time and thought, consist of energy. It has already been shown in Chapter 4 that with psychokinetic energy man can affect his physical body and objects external to him. This same energy in the form of thought can be used to construct specific events in everyday life.

Consider the possibility, since time is not absolute, that the future is a very fluid state. To illustrate, let us compare this fluidity with molten wax, capable of being molded into various forms. Then consider that thoughts projected onto this molten wax can act as molds that shape the wax according to the will of the individual. Thoughts are not abstract fantasies that possess no true substance. Thoughts are things! They consist of energy patterns capable of affecting everything they contact. The energy of thought can be used as so many seeds sown now in order to produce a specific crop at a specific future time.

The implications of such a hypothesis are extremely far-reaching, for if this theory is correct it places on each individual the responsibility for either accepting things as they are or actively doing something to bring about the circumstances he wants. If one chooses passive acceptance he cannot reasonably complain that circumstances are not to his liking and are holding him back. If one chooses action he still has no grounds for complaint, because the energy of one's own

110

thoughts and the patterns that energy takes form the circumstances that surround one. If circumstances are not to a person's liking he has only to change his mental attitude and form a mental picture of the circumstances he wants in order to change his life situation.

The science of quatum physics has been used to research the nature of time. Scientists in this area have found evidence to suggest that time flows backward as well as forward, lending support to the belief that time is truly relative and the future truly fluid.

Scientists who have researched precognition and psychokinetic energy as they relate to control of future events have concluded that an individual may bring about a desired event in the future through the use of thought and psychokinetic energy patterns.

As an aid to understanding the concept of a fluid future let us use the analogy of a roll of film. Picture a camera that contains a roll of film capable of 12 exposures. Consider that three sections of this roll already have been exposed, leaving nine sections potentially capable of capturing any situation. If the person who takes the picture chooses, he may photograph a building, an indoor scene, a mountain scene, or the busy activity of rush-hour traffic. The film itself is capable of accepting for future presentation any of these scenes, but the one actually etched on each section is at the discretion of the individual who takes the pictures. Time is much like a roll of film. Exposed sections depict the past; sections being exposed reflect the present; sections capable of exposure at another time show the future. Thus the future is comparable to unexposed sections on a roll of film. Whatever appears in the future is determined by the desires of the photographer.

Scientifically it has been shown that many individuals have the ability to expose film in a camera by the sheer power of thought. Many reputable scientists have investigated this phenomenon in strict laboratory conditions and have concluded that it is indeed possible through thought to project an image which actually forms on a photographic plate or roll of film where there was no possibility of exposure through ordinary means. These facts should give the reader an appreciation for the power of his own thinking. The future ahead holds an infinite number of possible exposures. Each individual can create in his life the circumstances or prints he desires!

The reader should keep in mind that certain circumstances already have been thrust into the future by thought patterns emitted to this time. As no two things can occupy the same space at the same time, in constructing future events to one's liking it is to be expected that previous events that are taking shape will be torn down. A perfect example is the student who has directed all the energy of his thoughts toward a career in business and then has decided to reconstruct his future and has begun to visualize circumstances that will permit him to enter medical school.

Whenever a person attempts to reconstruct his future he may have to deal with the emotional reactions of people who have already responded to the earlier patterns of thought. This change in lifestyle and goals may find family members or business partners confused or angry as they are confronted with the new circumstances. Therefore, one should not be surprised if during the reordering of a previously implanted event he experiences some discomfort in possibly having to deal with the reactions of other people concerned with those events up to this point. Reconstruction is generally for the purpose of building something better, and the concept of building a future with thought should be considered in the same way.

Rebuilding and new construction of thoughts always should be for a constructive purpose; otherwise great havoc can result. This warning is of utmost importance and must be considered seriously. In the construction of future events, thoughts are an actual and powerful method of bringing circumstances into one's life! We caution the reader not to underestimate this technique in considering the simplicity of the methodology behind it. It works, and it works with great accuracy. Don't make the mistake of using it as a toy, for it is capable of rearranging every area of life!

The dangers inherent in the technique are illustrated in the story of a young female Georgia

State student who despite the cautions decided to visualize a young man—who had to this point shown her no special attention—entering her life in a significant way and showering her with special concern.

One week later the young woman reported that after a week of visualization the young man had asked her for three dates during the past week. She was delighted and at the same time astounded that the technique had worked so quickly. Three months later at a college in Macon, Georgia, this same young woman appeared and asked how to visualize the young man out of her life. She said that his special concerns were driving her to distraction! He was, in fact, so solicitous of her well-being that together they had managed to demolish her social life.

The young woman could only again reorder her life by creating new circumstances around it. She would have to deal with the young man's reactions and the discomfort that would be engendered by the reordering. It is safe to say that the woman will never again take this method so lightly. She will consider the harvest well and long before using thought to seed a fluid future for desired events.

Not all people who attempt to use this method err on the side of overenthusiasm. Some individuals who attempt to build future events undermine their efforts with countless doubts and such statements as "Well, if it works ..." or "Do you really think something so simple can work?" This pessimism is analogous to building the foundation for a house in the morning and chipping away at it in the afternoon.

The technique should be seen for what it is; there is nothing magical about it. It involves only the use of mental and psychokinetic energy as a stamp to imprint on the fluidity of the future the events one wants to occur. It is composed, not of the ingredients in a magic formula or potion, but only of the nature of time in relation to the energy patterns of thought.

It is important that the reader appreciate that the energy patterns of thought are pseudomagnetic in quality. One does not attract the opposite of what one thinks about; instead, one's thoughts attract similar conditions. More simply, one gets what one gives, whether it is in the form of thoughts or of actions. Each person creates his own future by attracting to himself persons, actions, and circumstances that reflect his thought patterns.

This attraction may explain the loser cycle seen so much today in our society. Employers and major institutions spend millions of dollars yearly to motivate employees and management personnel to think constructively. Sad, but true indeed, is that most of this money is spent in vain. Pep rallies and rah-rah seminars never will produce a lasting effect on attitudes and thought patterns. An explanation of the dynamics underlying the process of

115

visualization would be much more advantageous to businesses, institutions, and society as a whole.

A person who is turned on to the power within himself and knows that he needs no magic words or formulas to achieve success will have no need for pep rallies. The person who is taught that his own mind is the most powerful force in the creation of his future, who is in touch with the laws for the beneficial use of this force becomes a truly self-motivating and self-actualizing individual.

Needless to say that to begin such training in childhood would allow derivation of positive benefits over a much longer period of time. People also would not need to relinquish childhood attitudes and thought patterns that inclined them toward the loser's cycle as adults. How much more simple for both teacher and student to have only to teach and learn what is necessary rather than having to correct past teachings not conducive to the achievement of life goals before proceeding with a pragmatic constructive approach.

The ideal definition of education may be stated simply as teaching in such a way that the material presented will not have to be cast off in the future. If we could present to our children the concept that thoughts are real things and bring about direct and often immediate reaction, we might then have a society much less bent toward chaotic situations—a society comprised of people who recognize that today's thoughts become tomorrow's actions and circumstances. Such people might be considered more sane because they realize that thought is creative energy in motion, and they accept responsibility for circumstances that exist in their lives, society, and the world. Someone once said, "The longest journey begins with the first step." We would add to this that everything that exists began with a thought!

Since the energy of thought is such a powerful force in our world, the individual who uses the process of visualization should understand that it must be done with accuracy. Our thoughts find material form exactly as they are sent out. An illustration of this need for accuracy is an incident that occurred in the life of a Georgia State University student who disregarded the caution.

After learning the technique of visualization the young student planned to use the method to attract to herself a man with the precise qualities she desired. She visualized a man who was extremely masculine, very decisive, interested in art, tall, handsome, and highly intelligent. Ten days later while performing the very unromantic task of taking out the garbage, she was approached by a man who lived in her apartment complex. He was tall, good-looking, extremely masculine, and intelligent. He asked if he could speak with her later that evening, and she agreed.

At this later meeting the man told the young woman that he was terribly attracted to her and wanted her to see him regularly. When the woman

117

mentioned that she knew he was married and living with his wife, he saw this as only a minor obstacle. She did not, and explained to him that although she was flattered by his attention she felt too many "minor obstacles" lay in their path to becoming better acquainted. Among these obstacles was the span between her 24 years and this charming gentleman's 82 years. The man certainly fulfilled every aspect of her visualization, but she had forgotten to visualize his age and marital state.

The situation was straightened out, and the young woman was able to see the element of comedy. She vows, however, to be much more cautious in using visualization in the future.

We want to emphasize that visualization is much more than a trend toward positive thinking; it involves the realization that natural laws are responsible for its efficiency, and it requires that one act as if the visualized circumstances were already a reality. For this reason submerged doubts tear away at constructive visualization.

Visualization requires that one visualize the desired circumstances at least three times a day. This repetition adds momentum to the energy of thought released into a fluid future. If one plans to bring specific circumstances into one's life but visualizes these circumstances only three or four times before discontinuing the practice, he may ask, "What happens to the energy of the thoughts released?" Without the momentum gained through repetition, the energy previously released will be depleted and not sufficiently strong to mold the fluid future. This winding down process often explains why many people who begin visualization enthusiastically but stop visualizing after only three or four sessions never see their thoughts materialize.

Several important points should be made in summary. First, visualization is not a toy but a very sound procedure whose roots spring from the nature of time and energy. Second, there is no magic in any object or set of words. True power for creative action lies within the mind of each person. He has only to become aware of this force to be able to use it constructively. Third, the energy of our thoughts takes material form exactly as the thoughts were structured. Thus accuracy in visualization is extremely important.

Hopefully the force of visualization will become a powerful tool for constructive purposes in your life and you will begin to teach the technique to your own children or to those for whom you are in some way responsible. Do not use visualization without serious thought and due consideration of the circumstances you are attempting to bring about in your life, to paraphrase a well-known comedian, "What you visualizes is what you gets!"

Visualization Exercises

VISUALIZATION THROUGH THOUGHT ALONE

1. You must have in your mind a clear picture of the circumstances you want to see materialize.

2. Give proper consideration to the outcome of the materialization of such circumstances in order to make certain that their material creation will be beneficial and constructive in your life.

3. Perform the breath exercises detailed in Chapter 1. Breath adds energy and momentum to the power of thought.

4. With eyes closed, visualize the circumstances you want to bring about by seeing them in your mind's eye, as if they were already a reality in material form.

5. Continue this visualization process for at least one full minute. As you increase your ability for concentration and visualization, the visualization process may be extended to two minutes.

6. This process should be repeated at least three and no more than five times a day. The

process should be carried on until the circumstances being visualized have taken material form.

7. Materialization of circumstances generally takes from five days to one month, depending on the complexity in construction of such circumstances and whether the individual allowed any doubts, which automatically slow down the materialization process.

VISUALIZATION THROUGH MENTAL MOVIES

1. After you have given time and consideration to the desirability of a circumstance you want to bring about in your life, you are ready to produce a mental motion picture that depicts those circumstances.

2. In this process you become script writer, director, and producer of a mental film that portrays your own future.

3. Perform the breath exercises outlined in Chapter 1.

4. In a comfortable position and with eyes closed, construct a mental image that contains the people and circumstances to be included in your visualization.

5. Mentally construct the scene—for example, office setting, home situation—in which the characters in your mental film are to interact.

6. Have a clear picture of the people to be included in this scene.

7. Since you write the script, mentally see

and hear each individual speaking your words and other people reacting to these spoken words exactly as you would have them react. For example, if you want to visualize being promoted at your place of employment, the mental film you produce might run as follows. You may visualize yourself at your desk, speaking with an employee directly over you in the chain of command. You will hear the employee say, "Mr. Smith wants to see you in his office, I think he has good news for you." Then you will hear yourself say "Thanks a lot," and see yourself leave your desk and walk to your superior's office.

On entering the office you will hear yourself say, "Mr. Jones said you wanted to see me, sir." With a clear picture of Mr. Smith seated at his desk you will hear Mr. Smith say, "Yes, George, I did. I have some good news for you. You're being promoted to the head of your department. The increase in pay and your new duties will start tomorrow. We have been very pleased with your performance in the past, and we know you will do a good job for us in this position in the future." You will then hear yourself respond, "Thank you very much, Mr. Smith. I appreciate your confidence, and I know I will do a good job for the company." The mental movie can stop here, since this would signify completion of the circumstances desired.

8. The mental film should be run at least three and no more than five times per day until the desired circumstances have materialized.

VISUALIZATION WITH THE AID
OF PHOTOGRAPHS

1. This form of visualization is particularly effective for the attainment of some material item you want to bring into your life. As before, you should consider well what changes the acquisition of such an item might bring into your life.

2. After performing the exercises in breathing techniques you should assume a relaxed position and mentally construct an image of the object you want to acquire.

3. A photograph of the object itself, or one that reflects such an object, is a helpful tool in visualization by this method.

4. Place the photograph or photographs in an envelope. It makes no difference whether the photograph has been cut from a magazine or is an actual print from a roll of film.

5. Use this picture to increase your ability to form a strong mental image of the object you want. After performing the prescribed breath techniques and while seated in a comfortable position, look at the photograph with full concentration for approximately 30 seconds. Then close your eyes and see yourself in possession of that particular item; for example, if the object is an automobile you may have cut an automobile advertisement from a magazine. After concentrating on the picture, in order to present the image clearly to your mind close your eyes and see yourself behind the wheel, driving down your own street. Visualize yourself

parking the car in front of your own house or apartment and hearing someone say, "Nice car . . . when did you get it?" Then hear yourself respond, "I just got it today. It's a real beauty isn't it?"

6. This process of visualization, as in the other exercises, should be performed at least three times and not more than five times per day until acquisition of the desired object becomes a reality.

This technique, especially advantageous to those who at first find it difficult to create and hold strong mental images, will facilitate the development of such an ability.

10 Ethics

Any reader who wants to research ethics can find innumerable books on the subject as well as innumerable books that discuss ethics along with other matters. The question of ethics has been considered by such people as Plato, Aristotle, Thomas Aquinas, Teilhard de Chardin, J. Krishnamurti, and countless others. If all the names were listed they would form a book.

The question of ethics penetrates every area of human life. The laborer, the college student, and the scientist all find themselves at one time or another confronted with ethics in the form of moral values. Although moral values may vary slightly from nation to nation some seem almost universal in civilized societies. Most cultures respect life and value the individual's right to privacy. As progress brings change, mankind faces the same ethical questions faced in the past and dealt with according to the circumstances and laws that existed at that time in the society.

What reader has not seen a movie or read a book concerned in some way, perhaps a major way, with the ethical problems scientists face? What reader in the civilized world today has not at some time actively participated in or actively listened to a discussion of the moral question involved in the use of nuclear energy and warfare?

The cheers that went up when Japan surrendered and World War II ended were followed in time by the often-asked question: "Were we as a nation morally justified in dropping the atomic bomb on Hiroshima and Nagasaki?" Some were quick to point an accusing finger at the scientist in an attempt to place responsibility on those who had made possible the use of such a device. We shall not argue here for or against justification in the atomic bombing of these two Japanese cities but shall deal with the question of scientific responsibility for such an event.

Progress brings with it many changes to which man must adjust his mode of thinking and behaving. In considering the question of right and wrong, good and bad, blessing or curse, the reader should look within this mode of response to progress, for here man makes a choice of how and to what ends he will use the tools science gives him. No discovery or material object is good or bad in or of itself. Good and evil enter our world in the uses

126

to which men put discoveries and material objects. When an individual or a nation makes a conscious choice to use a law, an object, or a theory in a way they know to be hurtful to others, either by infringing on their human rights or by doing them bodily harm, that choice has introduced evil into the world.

People who are aware of the potential good a specific scientific discovery may offer ask another question that attempts to place on science responsibility for the results of progress: "What about people who will use this discovery in the wrong way?" In answer to this question it must be pointed out that everything that exists could be used "in the wrong way." Every new discovery, mankind's every progressive step, is in danger of being used by some people in a way that proves hurtful to others.

Agriculture, which began to be used extensively about 8,000 years ago, is an example of just such a giant step in human progress. Most readers surely would agree that food cultivation is one of man's greatest blessings. Progress in agriculture has allowed the world to feed its people; nations with more advanced agricultural techniques teach these techniques and/or sell food to nations not so advanced.

Scientists now are looking for ways to introduce the techniques of agriculture to ocean beds so that in the future earth may be able to produce sufficient food to feed its growing population. People are looking hopefully to agriculture for the answer to the question: "How can we have enough food to feed our growing numbers on this planet?"

These same people who look to agriculture with such hope may never have considered that not until the advent of agriculture did land become an extremely valuable commodity that caused men to fight army against army, nation against nation for the right to its possession. Class distinctions were created as society divided into those who owned and those who worked the land and, later, into those who made and those who sold implements to till the soil. Many people became wealthy—some at the expense of their neighbors. All this fragmentation of a society previously without agriculture was brought about by the uses and purposes to which men applied its discovery. Will the reader now attempt to answer the question: "Is agriculture a blessing or a curse?" With the history of agriculture in mind one can see that a cut and dried answer, a simple yes or no, is hardly possible.

This example shows that each new discovery is like a two-sided coin. Just as no one-sided coins exist, so nothing is known to man that cannot by his discretion and choice be misused. Perhaps the better part of valor in attempting to answer the blessing-or-curse question is to weigh the potentially good uses of a new discovery against the number of people in the world who will misuse the same discovery. It is not reasonable to call an end to discovery in order to correct such misuse. It is more feasible to educate and train people in such a way that they will choose to use scientific discoveries in a manner beneficial to mankind.

The relevance of ethics to the science of parapsychology becomes clear when one recognizes the powerful significance of discoveries in this field. The ability to communicate mind to mind or through clairvoyance to possess specific facts about both the past and the future is threatening to some people who view these abilities as potentially capable of infringing on their right to privacy. We emphasize again that no ability is in and of itself good or bad. Some people may, and most likely will, misuse their talents.

One of the greatest forces available to mankind against such misuse is education of the general public in parapsychology. Through mass education we can prevent this knowledge from becoming the esoteric possession of a few individuals or nations. Through education and by encouraging people to develop parapsychological abilities within themselves we can also reduce the number of persons who make a lucrative living by using such abilities to entertain or advise. People who seek advice are willing to pay someone they believe is special or gifted.

There will always be those who have developed these abilities more fully than others, just as there are those who play the piano for their own enjoyment and those who play well enough to give a concert. However, through general education and knowledge we can help the public to distinguish among those who have developed their abilities as has the concert pianist. People so educated will be able to recognize those who offer much and deliver little as they become financially well off.

The person who seeks clairvoyant information owes to himself an ethical obligation that consists of his responsibility to investigate as far as possible the qualifications of the clairvoyant or psychic. The public can greatly curtail fraudulent psychics by being discriminating in those they seek out and prices they are willing to pay.

Each person is always responsible to himself in any area that involves dependence on another. Frauds can make a living by commercializing their abilities, real or imaginary, because many people are willing to shed decision-making responsibilities by happily following the advice of one who supposedly knows best. Some readers may be astounded to learn about some of the advice supposedly intelligent people seek from so-called psychics who set up businesses beside highways or main thoroughfares. Questions include: Will I take a trip this summer? Should I sell my house? Should I change jobs? Should I marry the person I'm dating? Will my husband and I straighten out our marital problems? And the winner of all questions: Should we get a divorce? When one considers that 99 percent of these wayside psychics have had no training in vocational guidance, marriage counseling, or psychotherapy, it is more than a little frightening to know that people make decisions based on what these psychics tell them.

A much needed regulatory body composed of persons qualified in both parapsychology and counseling or psychotherapy could maintain a register of persons who practice in various fields of the psychic sciences. The register would include their qualifications in the field in which they claim expertise, and this information could be made available to the public on request. As a sort of better business bureau this regulatory body could also keep a list of complaints registered against any persons who claim to give psychic information or advice. Any person's inclusion on the register would be a voluntary matter. This register would be an attempt to maintain ethical standards and protect the public; so ethical practitioners interested in doing both would gladly allow themselves to be listed.

Such a register is being formed now through Psychic Science Institute, a nonprofit organization dedicated to research and education. Psychic Science Institute in Atlanta, Georgia, will accept applications from people throughout the country. This register is not the ultimate answer to the ethical question of the qualification of those in the psychic sciences, but it is a constructive move away from destructive criticism about what has not been done!

The future holds great promise for new developments through the science of parapsychology. With the research already in progress in dermaoptics, the future hopefully will bring these techniques to the point where they can benefit all of the world's blind, visually handicapped, and slow readers. Man does not exist to serve science; science exists to serve man! How better can science serve than to give the knowledge and techniques that enable men to discover and enrich their own human potential?

This is the promise of parapsychology.

Index

C

D

E

J

K

M

N

O

Object reading. *See* Psychometry
Occultists, 6, 32, 62, 103
Oracle of Delphi, 2, 47, 48
Osis, Dr. Karlis, 23
Oxford University, 49

P

Parapsychology, 2, 23, 37, 40, 49, 74, 75–76, 101,
    129, 131, 132
Past events, 1, 2, 3, 5, 6, 10, 19–20, 109, 112
Periscope, 2
Plato, 125
Present events, 1, 2, 5, 6, 112
Psychic Science Institute, 131
Psychokinesis (PK), 37–45, 110, 111, 115
    exercises, 41–45
Psychometry, 5–8, 17–20, 24
Psychotherapy, 100–101, 131

R

Rahn, Dr. Otto, 30
Reincarnation, 61–76
    doctrines, 62–68
    scientific views of, 68–76
Rhine, Dr. Louisa, 2, 38, 49
Rhine, Dr. J. B., 2, 23–24, 38–39, 49
Russia, 2, 22, 30, 31, 38, 78

S

St. Augustine, 99
Schopenhauer, Arthur, 49
Scientific American, 48
Socrates, 50
Stanford University, 30
Swedenborg, Emanuel, 48–49

T

Telepathy, 13, 14, 21–27, 56, 83, 97, 101
  exercises, 25–27
Three Faces of Eve, 57
Transmigration of souls, 62

U

Universal ether, 1–2, 56
Universal unconscious, 1. *See also* Meditation

V

Verification, 8–9, 10, 18, 24, 27, 29, 34–35, 36, 39, 51–52,
    54, 56, 57–59, 70–76, 112
Vibrations, 3–4, 5, 7
Visualization, 109–24
  exercises, 120–24

Y

Yale University, 2
Yoga, 1–2, 32, 62, 75, 95–98

About the Authors

Evelyn M. Monahan teaches parapsychology at the Georgia State University School of Special Studies. She did her undergraduate work at the University of Tennessee, where she majored in psychology. Later, she attended Emory University, doing graduate work in experimental psychology.

Ms. Monahan has appeared on numerous television and radio shows, lectured extensively, and written articles for business magazines.

Her professional activities include working with the handicapped, especially the blind, the deaf, and the learning disabled.

Terry Bakken is woman's editor and a staff writer on a newspaper, and has done free-lance work.

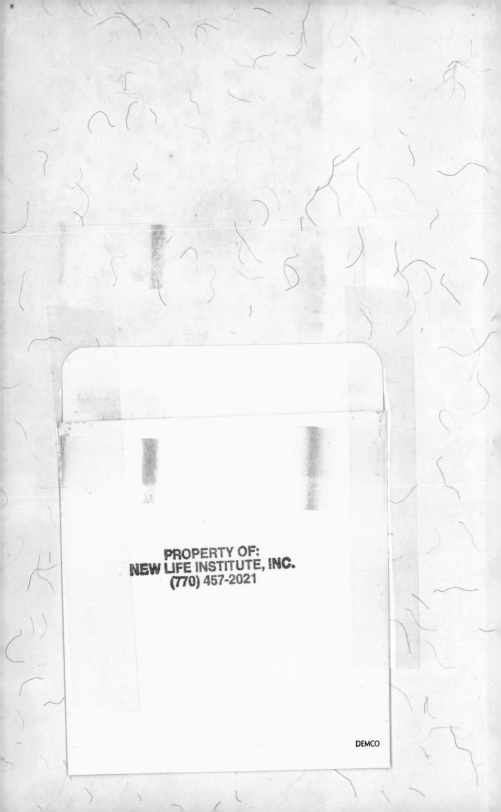